A Community Guide to Social Impact Assessment
2015 Fourth Edition

Rabel J. Burdge

Burdge, Rabel J.

A Community Guide to Social Impact Assessment: 2015 Fourth Edition
by Rabel J. Burdge.
p. cm.
Includes bibliographical references.
Preassigned LCCN: 93-087340.
ISBN 0-941042-17-0

1. Social indicators. 2. Technological innovations -- Social aspects -- Evaluation.
3. Social prediction. I. Title.

HN25.S57 1983   303.4'83
                              QBI94-680

Society and Natural Resources Press ™
IASNR
Box 2446, Suite 270 SHSU
Huntsville, Texas 77341
USA
(936) 337-8589

Printed in the United States of America

Table of Contents

Available Companion Materials

FOREWORD

Social impact assessment (SIA) emerged in the early 1970s as an applied social science field in response to the need to understand the impacts on human populations of natural resource developments and environmental policy alternatives. The impetus was the passing of the National Environmental Policy Act of 1969 (NEPA) by the U.S. Congress. The first meeting of practitioners and academics on social impact assessment was convened by C. P. Wolf in the fall of 1973 at the annual meeting of Environmental Design Research Associates (EDRA) held in Milwaukee, Wisconsin. Sue Johnson and Rabel Burdge presented the paper *Social Impact Assessment: A Tentative Approach* at that first meeting. Twenty-one years later, in the spring of 1994, the Interorganizational Committee on Guidelines and Principals for Social Impact Assessment published *Guidelines and Principals for Social Impact Assessment* intended for U.S. federal agencies who wished to incorporate social impact assessment into their NEPA procedures. The Interorganizational Committee revised the document in 2003 and published it as *Principles and Guidelines for Social Impact Assessment. International Guidelines and Principles for Social Impact Assessment* were published in 2010 by the International Association for Impact Assessment. By the 21st Century, social impact assessment was a recognized sub-field of the social science disciplines of sociology, geography, political science, anthropology, psychology and the design and planning arts. SIA is now an integral part of integrated environmental management and the importance of public involvement as a component of social impact assessment is recognized by planners, resource managers and legislators alike.

Organization of the Book

This book is laid out in workbook format in order that the user, with the aid of an instructor or a workshop facilitator, can do a social impact assessment on a proposed project, plan or projected policy change at the community and regional level. The margins are wide allowing for comments on the SIA process and the proposed action being assessed. The book is a *working draft* and will be updated as needed.

Definition, History and the Concepts of Social Impact Assessment The first three chapters outline the field of SIA and how it evolved in the context of environmental assessment, environmental planning, and project evaluation. It concludes by outlining the concepts used by social scientists in organizing the research and practice of social impact assessment. The reader may skim these chapters and for more details, locate the companion books: ***The Concepts, Process and Methods of Social Impact Assessment: Rabel J. Burdge and Colleagues***, by Rabel J. Burdge and ***Social Assessment: Theory, Process and Techniques*** by C. Nicholas Taylor, Hobson Bryan and Colin Goodrich both published in the 3$^{rd \cdot}$ Edition by the Social Ecology Press, now the Society and Natural Resources Press, in 2004.

Doing Social Impact Assessment in the Project Setting Chapters 4-6 help the reader focus on identifying a community level project (policy) for doing a social impact assessment. Included in these chapters are steps in the **SIA process**, procedures for doing **scoping, profiling** and **identifying stakeholders**, how to **determine project boundaries**, and **sources of data and information** to do the SIA.

The Social Impact Assessment Variables outline in Chapters 7-11 provide detailed instructions for obtaining data and evaluating the importance and significance of 28 social impact assessment variables organized under the five categories of: Population Impacts, Community and Institutional Change, Communities in Transition, Individual and Family Level Impacts, and Community and Infrastructure Needs.

Identifying and Summarizing Significant Social Impacts. Chapter 12 provides a worksheet to consolidate and rank the most significant social impacts.

Chapter 13 outlines a *Community Level Approach to Mitigation, Monitoring* and a *Social Impact Management Plan (SIMP)* for submission to a licensing agency in conjunction with the Integrated Environmental Impact assessment (IEIA)

Chapter 14 on *Impacts and Benefits Agreements* provides some legal direction for the impacted communities facing significant biophysical and social impacts to benefit from a proposed development.

The *Appendix Material* includes a social impact assessment bibliography organized by topic, and websites helpful in doing social impact assessment.

Rabel J Burdge is a *Professor Emeritus* at the University of Illinois at Urbana-Champaign where he held tenure appointments from 1975 to 1996 in the Institute for Environmental Studies and the Departments of Agricultural Economics (Rural Sociology), Leisure Studies (Parks and Recreation) and Urban and Regional Planning. He is also an *Adjunct Professor* in the Department of Sociology and Huxley College of the Environment at Western Washington University in Bellingham, where he taught courses on environmental sociology and social impact assessment from 1996-2012.

In 2003, Burdge edited a double issue of the international journal, *Impact Assessment and Project Appraisal,* Volume 21 (2&3) titled, "The Practice of Social Impact Assessment" and in 2004 completed the 3rd edition of his two SIA textbooks: *The Concepts, Process and Methods of Social impact Assessment* and *A Community Guide to Social Impact Assessment*, both update for publication in 2004 by the Social Ecology Press (now the Society and Natural Resources Press) of Middleton, Wisconsin and recently purchased by the International Association for Society and Natural Resources (IASNR). The 4th Edition of *A Community Guide to Social Impact Assessment* was published in 2015. In addition to the above books, Burdge is author of *Coping with Change: an Interdisciplinary Impact Assessment of the Lake Shelbyville Reservoir.*

In 1990 he was elected the President of the International Association for Impact Assessment (IAIA) and in 1994 received from IAIA the Rose-Hulman Institute of Technology Award for outstanding contributions to the field of impact assessment

Recent consultancies include: 2001--preparation of the Social Impact Assessment manual for the Bureau of Reclamation, US Department of Interior; 2002--international expert for UNEP-Malaysia on the preparation of SIA guidelines; and 2003--preparation of Principles and Guidelines for Social Impact Assessment for the US National Marine Fisheries Service (NOAA).

Annually, Burdge gives training courses on social impact assessment for such professional organizations as the International Association for Impact Assessment (IAIA) and the International Association for Society and Natural Resources (IASNR) where he received the *Lifetime Achievement Award*, and the Rural Sociological Society (RSS) where he received the *Distinguished Rural Sociologist Award* in 1996. He has also given training courses on social impact assessment for the following private sector companies and organizations: Worley-Parsons, Calgary, Alberta; Statoil (National Oil Company of Norway); ConocoPhillips in Calgary; The Cree Nation of Northern Quebec, Montreal, Quebec and Pemex (National Oil Company) in Villahermosa, Mexico; Magellan Corporate Strategies of Calgary, Alberta; and the Inter-American Development Bank in Washington, D.C.

How to Use the *Community Guide to Social Impact Assessment*

❧ The *Guide* is designed to walk you through doing an actual social impact assessment for some development event or project affecting your community.

❧ Chapters 1-3 provide a background and history about SIA. Some of this material is redundant so you may skim it unless you are big on SIA history.

❧ Chapters 3-6 deal with the SIA process and are designed to get you started.

❧ The 28 exercises in Chapters 7-11 will help you collect information begin to understand social impacts.

❧ In my experience, an empirical indicator of social impacts not only helps decision-makers to understand what a social impact is, but it helps convince them that the impact is real and deserves to be considered in the decision making process.

❧ Although, I provide indicators and some guidance about interpreting each SIA variable, you must do the actual tests of significance and interpret the results within the context of your project.

❧ The summaries at the end of each chapter are both a test over what you have learned and a summary of your progress in doing the SIA.

❧ Chapter 13 will help you design the mitigation, enhancement and monitoring program for identified significant social impacts and concludes with an outline of a Social Impact Assessment Management Plan (SIMP). Chapter 14 outlines impact benefit agreements.

❧ When you finish, your completed SIA should be written inside the covers of this workbook. The margins are designed so you can write in the workbook.

❧ Where possible, I have include helpful websites. However, websites change or are no longer available.

❧ The references listed at the end of the workbook may be downloaded, purchased, or are in the serialized literature available at many university libraries. The Utah State University in Logan, Utah, USA has circulating collection of Social Impact Assessment books and journals.

Chapter 1. Social Impact Assessment: What is it and Why Should We do it?

Objectives of this Book

We all need a crystal ball to help us predict the consequences of our decisions. This book helps citizens and community leaders, project proponents, planners and governmental officials at all levels understand and cope with the social changes which take place at the community level as they collectively plan for and deal with the opportunities and consequences of a proposed development project or policy change. The information to complete this *Guide* is available from local and regional governments that collect census and other data. The reasons for ***A Community Guide to Social Impact Assessment*** are twofold:

1. To explain why we do Social Impact Assessment by:

- Understanding how a proposed action will change the life of communities and regions;
- Alerting planners and proponents to likely social change;
- Including SIA as part of the community decision process;
- Providing empirical indicators of likely social impacts and determine those that are significant;
- Using the measurements of social change to understand and interpret the consequences of a <u>proposed action</u>;
- Outlining steps a community might take to mitigate and enhance the positive and minimize the negative consequences of change; and
- Explaining how a community benefits from the change that development brings.

2. And to strengthen community response to social change through a better understanding and awareness of its consequences so that change becomes a positive experience for your community by:

- Providing a strategy to involve all community members in responding to a proposed change or development;
- Acknowledging the negative consequences of change so you can deal with the situation in an open manner; and
- Seeking an approach to understand the importance of sociological, economic and psychological needs of community life.

In completing *The Guide to SIA*, you won't simply learn how to conduct a social impact assessment—you'll actually **do** it!

> *The social benefits and consequences of project development, consolidation, and closure (abandonment) always occur, can be measured, and are usually borne at the community and local level—but the rationale for projects and the decisions are justified and sold on the basis of regional and national economic goals!* ....Rabel J. Burdge, 1969

What is Social Impact Assessment?

Social Impact Assessment is a sub-field of the social sciences that has developed a knowledge base to provide a systematic analysis **in advance** of impacts on the day-to-day quality of life of persons and communities whose environment is affected by a proposed plan, program, project or policy change. *Social Impacts* (also effects and consequences) refers to changes to individuals and communities due to a **proposed action** that alters the way in which people live, work, play, relate to one another, organize to meet their needs and generally cope as members of society. We do social impact assessment to help individuals, communities, as well as government and private sector organizations understand and be able to anticipate the possible social consequences on human populations and communities of proposed projects or policy changes. SIA is done as part of the planning process and therefore alerts the **planner** and the **project proponent** (through the social assessor) to the likelihood of social impacts. Like a biological, physical, or economic impact—social impacts have to be pointed out and measured in order to be understood and communicated to the impacted population and responsible decision-makers. *Social impact assessment* provides a realistic appraisal of possible social ramifications and suggestions for project alternatives and possible mitigation measures.

When Do We Do Social Impact Assessment?

We do social impact assessment when we want to learn about and understand the consequences of a project, activity or policy on human populations and human communities. It may be for a big event, such as the construction of a highway through an urban neighborhood. It may be small, as for example, the closing of a hospital in a Filipino Village. It may be required by law, as in the case of the U.S. National Environmental Policy Act (NEPA), which is triggered when federal funds, land and legislation is involved. It may be seen as prudent, as for example, evaluating the benefits and consequences of more tourism at a sacred Maori site in New Zealand.

Who should use this book?

The *Guide* is written for community leaders, resource managers, elected officials, planners, project proponents, governmental and non-governmental change agents as well as extension and development workers in both developed and developing countries. It is written as a guide for the **social assessor** who will do or train others to do social impact assessment. The book is purposely published in *spiral or notebook* form because it is intended to be used as a workbook which will be updated as new research on possible social impacts becomes available. It is intended for persons who wish to use the results of a social impact assessment to help communities cope with and adjust to change. But most of all, it is written so the educated citizenry can understand how a new project or policy will change their lives.

Why the Interest in Social Impact Assessment?

Attempts at modernization in both Developed and Developing Countries have altered the physical environment, created untold economic problems as well as disrupting the lives of countless millions of the world's population. When the developments were few and the numbers of people small, concern was less and the impacts on life-sustaining ecosystems were fewer. However, accelerated population growth has brought the earth's resources and its people closer to sustainable limits. As a result, community leaders, policy makers, legislators, and the informed citizenry want to know the consequences and impacts of change prior to project approval.

> "Assessments of any kind…social, economic, technological, health, environmental, etc., are another way of saying *look before you leap!*"

The term *social impact assessment* was coined in the context of environmental impact analysis stemming from the U.S. National Environmental Policy Act (NEPA) of 1969, to recognize and quantify the impacts on human populations resulting from significant alteration of the bio-physical environment. Social impact assessment differs from other types of social science analysis in that it is ***anticipatory***. The goal is to measure and interpret the consequences of a proposed action before it actually takes place. The inclusion of social impact assessment as a component of the decision making process means that project evaluation must consider the effects and consequences for human populations.

Doing social impact assessment deals not only with process (how to do it) but what social impacts mean for the affected community. In this *Guide*, I identify social impact variables that are likely to occur, define them in a matter that is understandable, show how they can be measured and demonstrate how each may be understood in a project setting. The goal is to provide a readable, usable and understandable approach to social impact assessment and demonstrate how it fits the practical needs of the planning process. The concepts, process and methods of SIA can be applied to development projects around the world, but by necessity, the examples are drawn from the author's experience in the U.S., Canada, Australia, New Zealand, Malaysia, South Africa and The Netherlands.

For much of the foreseeable future, large scale development and the resulting environmental and technological impacts will take place in developing countries. Examples include the construction of coal fired and nuclear generators, water impoundments, mineral exploration and agricultural expansion in previously forested or desert areas. Most of the funds for these activities will come from developed countries and bi-lateral aid, lending and donor agencies. Doing and using the results of an SIA will go a long way to "putting people first" in the final decision before project implementation (☛Cernea, 1991).

Are Social Impacts and Environmental Impacts Related?

The U.S. National Environmental Policy Act of 1969 (NEPA) was signed by then President Nixon on January 1, 1970. Under the new law, proponents of development projects that involved federal land, money or jurisdiction were required to file an environmental impact statement (EIS) detailing the impacts of the project on the environment. The EIS statement was also required to propose alternatives to the proposed action, consider mitigation measures for the impacts to the bio-physical environment and outline the monitoring program that would alert the community and proponents to any change in predicted social impacts.

> *"...now that we have dealt with the problem of the permafrost and the caribou and what we will do with hot oil, what about changes in the customs and ways of the Alaskan natives..."*
>
> Comments by native Alaskan Chief during the hearings on the Trans Alaska Oil Pipeline - 1970.

In February, 1970, the Department of the Interior submitted a six-page EIS statement to accompany the application for the Trans-Alaska pipeline permit. Two days later the Friends of the Earth and the Environmental Defense Fund filed suit contending that the Interior EIS statement failed to adequately deal with a host of environmental problems ranging from damage to the pipeline from the melting of the permafrost to the impact on the annual migration of several caribou herds due to the pipeline barrier. Residents of Fairbanks, Alaska also wondered out loud what could be done with all those construction workers that would flock north to work on the pipeline.

Three years later the permit to build the pipeline was issued. In the meantime, the EIS statement had grown from six pages to six feet. More importantly, most of the potential environmental damage had been dealt with and solved to the satisfaction of the courts, the environmentalists and the Alyeska Pipeline Company. Anticipatory planning had worked and all sides agreed that the NEPA process was key to dealing with issues that might otherwise not have been addressed. Starting in 1977, oil has been piped from Prudhoe Bay since 1977 with no major environmental damage to either the fauna or flora, that is, until the Exxon Valdez set sail on Prince William Sound in 1989.

Unfortunately, as one native chief pointed out, the impacts on both the native and non-native Alaskan people were never addressed. Would the traditional cultures and way of life be changed by so massive of a construction? What about the influx of transient workers who shared a different dialect of the English language and exhibited unfamiliar life styles. Obviously, with a total population of 351,000 (in 1973) the state of Alaska could provide only a small fraction of the estimated 42,000 persons that worked on the pipeline at its peak. Because of these and other related developments the concern for the social impact of development on the human populations emerged.

Who Participates in the SIA Process?

Project development and policy change brings together five collections of actors; the project proponent, the community, the SIA practitioner, the governmental regulatory unit (often proponent as well as decision maker) and the larger public—each with its own particular set of values, behaviors and interests. These individual and organizational agendas lead either to cooperation or conflict. The goals for SIA are to focus on and reduce the inherent conflict by equalizing or neutralizing the concentration of power through the provision of a communication network and providing the opportunity for an objective appraisal of the social impacts of a proposed action on the human environment.

Instructions: Your *Guide to SIA* has four citation formats

📖 ***Concepts,*** e.g. (Chapter 17) refers to a chapter in the companion book, ***The Concepts, Process and Methods of SIA***, 2004 by Rabel J. Burdge. The book is available in most university libraries and includes a Chinese translation: ISBN 978-7-5111-0612-4.

🖰 ***Website*** Means you may go to that site for more information. e.g.,
http://www.iaia.org/pdf/Key%20Citations_SIA%2014%20Apr.pdf

📄 Refers to ***Supporting Documents for SIA*** with directions for possible location.

🖛 Refers to citations listed in the bibliography and references at the end of this workbook, e.g., (🖛 Leistritz and Murdock, 1981*)*.

---

1. Proponent

In the U.S. the proponent is either a local, state or federal government agency such as the U.S. Army Corps of Engineers or the elected City Council or a private sector company (ranging in size from one that does apartment units to consortiums that build massive energy projects). The proponent acts: 1) as initiator of the project proposal and of the SIA process; 2) as evaluator and assessor, on whom the onus lies to conduct the SIA; and 3) as implementer, responsible to construct, operate and monitor the proposed action. In developing countries, the proponent is almost always the government (📖 *Concepts,* Chapter 20), an international bi-lateral lending or donor agency such as The World Bank or a multi-national corporation.

All proponents have vested interests (generally in making money) and likely will highlight only benefits and minimize any consequences or risks to local populations. As such, the SIA may not always be as complete as it could be or offer a truly in depth assessment of the situation.

On the other hand, doing SIA can help the proponent to understand the uncertain environment in which they are operating. For example, a detailed SIA would provide an accurate picture of the skill level of local labor as well as information on mitigation and/or compensatory measures that may be required. Should the costs appear to outweigh the benefits, the proposed action could be canceled or a potentially less risky alternative pursued. SIA can also become a means of enhancing the public image of the proponent. However, the big benefit is that the SIA process may uncover alternatives that achieve the same objectives at less cost with fewer impacts on the human and bio-physical environment.

2. Community (country, village, municipality, shire, etc.)

Concerned citizens and elected community leaders must play an active role in both the planning and SIA process. For example, in rural Illinois (USA), communities leaders have actually conducted their own social assessments of proposed projects. They saw the process as a way of better understanding their community and having a say in their future. It enhances community cohesion and allows community members to be active participants in the planning and decision making process (Concepts, Chapter 8).

3. Government Agencies

Examples include local shire and municipal councils, the U.S. Environmental Protection Agency (USEPA), Council on Environmental Quality (CEQ), and in Canada, the Canadian Environmental Assessment Administration. Outside North America, Ministries of the Environment are responsible for supervision of the EIA process. As law-maker and arbitrator of conflict, government insures equity, sets guidelines and policy, and enforces adherence to regulations. They review the assessment for future policy consideration, evaluate and make the final decision on permits. In addition to acting as regulator, evaluator and decision-maker, government could be called upon to assume additional roles, (technical directions, project leader, and interpreter of community concerns) to provide perspective and encourage planners and community residents to do SIAs. Government may be a project proponent, in which case another agency or the juridical system must ensure that the social impact assessment is adequately prepared.

4. The SIA Practitioner

The social impact assessor (practitioner) is hired by the proponent (or the government agency) to do the research, prepare the SIA statement and facilitate the public participation process. That person (or organization) acts as an interpreter and mediator, translating for all involved a "definition" of the situation and seeking out approaches and solutions which bring the proponent and community together on any conflicting issues. In many cases SIA statements are done by consulting firms under contract to the proponent. The SIA practitioner may work with the impacted community with funds provided by a local, provincial, or regional government (Buchan, 2003).

5. The Larger Public

By public, we mean *all* interested citizens to include members of such non-governmental organizations (NGOs), e.g. Chambers of Commerce, the Tourism and Convention Bureau, environmental advocates such as the Sierra Club and the Audubon Society, local civic clubs such as Kiwanis, agricultural organizations and local cooperatives—to name but a few. In some countries they are called interested and affected parties. These concerned citizens and organizations often raise issues in public meetings or hearings that have not been properly addressed by the project proponent, the government, elected leaders or even the SIA practitioner. The public involvement process (📖 *Concepts*, Chapter 17) is a way for the interested public to be involved in the planning process and bring alternatives to the attention of the proponent and the government.

Participatory and Analytical Social Impact Assessment

Is it participative or is it analytical? Does the practitioner (social assessor) help the impacted communities "participate" in, understand and adjust to anticipated changes? Or does the assessor work from a detached, "analytical" perspective—only reporting to the decision agency the likely social impacts resulting from a proposed action?

The *analytical approach* to SIA assumes that social change is ubiquitous, but that a new project or policy alters the normal flow of social change. Furthermore, this approach stresses that impact events will vary in specificity, intensity, duration, and a variety of other factors. It then becomes important to understand what the social impacts of a particular development will be rather than only being aware, in general, that social change will take place. This approach also assumes that social impacts are most observable at the local or community level—at least the direct effects. For most social impact variables the measuring and interpretation works best the more restricted the area of study. For example, the rapid influx of construction workers is easily observed and predictable, but the gradual shifting of power from old-timers to newcomers or even a new government agency is less obvious and more difficult to measure. From the analytical perspective the goal for the assessor becomes one of identifying, measuring, and understanding the consequences of change for human populations—given different types of impact events (📖 *Concepts*, Chapter 7).

To Buchan, the *participative approach*…"includes interested and affected parties in deciding indicators and measures of environmental and social impacts, in evaluation of effects and monitoring." She goes on to point out that involving…"communities in a participatory manner facilitates skill transfer, fosters buy-in and creates local social capital (📖 Buchan, 2003:168-9)." Participatory social impact assessment is not public consultation or public participation in that the process goes beyond asking the public for input or even involving them in the decision process. It is including the community in problem identification, design, project implementation, and monitoring. Implicit in the participative approach is the notion of understanding social change through experience. The focus is more on social action, with emphasis on helping the impacted population adjust to impending change. Being sensitive to the existence of possible social impacts is as important as actually being able to identify them. An important by-product for participants is an awareness and understanding of how their community works.

The best approach is a combination of the *analytical* and *participatory*. By utilizing past social science research, the assessor is better able to understand what is likely to happen to human populations given different impact events. The participative approach allows the impacted community to participate in and take possession of the assessment. Remember that:

> *The practical goal of social impact assessment is to anticipate likely areas of impact, to utilize the information in the planning process, and to plan appropriate mitigation.*

Who Should Use *A Community Guide to Social Impact Assessment*?

1. Present and future natural resource managers in state, provincial and federal agencies will need to know how to apply SIA within the context of an Environmental Assessment. Graduates for these positions come from departments of forestry, parks and recreation, fish and wildlife, water resource management, and conservation, as well as other biological and natural resource related programs. Environmental planning will be more beneficial if social impact assessment actually becomes an integrated component.

2. Community Development workers and Cooperative Extension, county or local level agricultural agents, natural resource conservation employees, county and local government regulators should use this *Guide*. In short, it would be advantageous to all professional (paid and volunteer) change agents who work with local communities and municipalities on a regular basis. These people need to understand how project development affects their communities.

3. Persons that work in developing countries with, for example, USAID (U.S. Agency for International Development) and the World Bank will need this book. A *"National"* from a developing country who gets involved with foreign assistance will also need to know about SIA. The *International Principles or SIA* will help in this setting (📖 *Concepts*, Chapter 23).

4. Students in Departments of Landscape Architecture, Architecture, Urban and Regional Planning, Environmental Studies, Forestry, Recreation and Parks as well as social science departments need to understand how social impact

assessment and the anticipatory planning process fit together. Advanced undergraduate and master's level students from environmental engineering, geology, or biological sciences would benefit from and should insist that SIA be part of a general course on the human consequences of technological change.

5. It is possible to get a job as an SIA practitioner with either a federal or state agency or international donor agency, but more likely with a consulting firm that does EIAs. However, SIA responsibilities are often lumped with public involvement, community relations, and general environmental planning activities.

When is Social Impact Assessment "*Required*"?

The utilization and implementation of social impact assessment has moved forward in an uneven manner among U.S. federal agencies and is not specifically required in the Canadian Environmental Assessment Act. The numbers of environmental impact statements completed by agencies beyond the initial environmental assessment has diminished in recent years, thereby limiting the opportunity to do SIA. Furthermore, the practice of social impact assessment at the federal level has been hindered by the unfortunate equating of social impact assessment with public participation and public involvement (↜ Burdge, 2002). Public involvement techniques have been well developed and are utilized by the land management agencies that prepare large numbers of EIS statements. Unfortunately, administrators tend to think that doing public involvement also meets the requirements for social impact assessment. A further problem is the absence of legal mandates specifically requiring SIA statements. While the original NEPA legislation required that social (human) impacts be considered, the updated 1986 CEQ guidelines do not specifically mandate it. However, in developing environmental assessment procedures, most agencies have included SIA requirements in their operational manuals (▢ *Concepts*, Chapters 6 and 12).

> "SIA may not always be required by law, but proponents who do it will have better and more acceptable projects in the long run."

Social Impact Assessment as Sociological Practice

The objective of the SIA is to anticipate and predict social impacts in advance so that the assessor's recommendation becomes part of the decision making and planning process. However, sociological researchers have given scant attention to identifying, measuring and understanding sociological concepts in advance of the event.

Most sociologists and anthropologists would probably say that SIA is what we have been doing all along. Rural sociology, for example, has a rich tradition of community/social change research that provides a large body of findings about how rural communities adjust to outside influences. Applied anthropology rightly claims that they have always studied social impacts particularly where indigenous and modern cultures meet. Such titles as…*Is SIA old wine in new bottles?* reinforce the notion that SIA is really a re-labeling of what we have done all along (Tester and Mykes, 1979).

However, sociology and the applied components of other social science disciplines provide valuable input by doing the follow-up (ex-post facto) research and monitoring projects that provide the knowledge base for SIA. Only in such a manner will we be able to learn about likely social impacts given different policy and project settings.

Review of Chapter One

1. Social impact assessment is: _____

_____

2. Name the one factor assessments of all kinds share? (e.g., health, social, economic)

_____

3. Major uses and importance of social impact assessments are:

a. To help citizens understand the consequences of project development.
b. To uncover alternatives in achieving project/policy goals.
c. To understand impacts and change in advance of the event.
d. To maximize the benefits and minimize the costs of social change.
e. All of the above.

4. **T or F** All U.S. federal land management agencies, the United Nations and the World Bank have developed procedures for doing social impact assessment within the Guidelines provided by the International Association for Impact Assessment (IAIA).

5. **T or F** Social and environmental impact assessments are almost always initiated by concerned local citizens.

Chapter 2 provides a *History of Social Impact Assessment*. You may skip it and go to Chapter 3 on *A Social Impact Assessment Model* or you may go directly to Chapter 4, *Getting Started* if you want to begin your SIA project.

On to Chapter Two

Chapter 2. The History and Importance of Social Impact Assessment

The purpose of Chapter 2 is to provide you with:

- A history of the U.S. National Environmental Policy Act (NEPA)
- How social impact assessment got started
- Some key events in the history of social impact assessment
- How social impact assessment fits the planning process, and
- A brief look at some of the conceptual problems in doing social impact assessment.

Before social and environmental impact assessment started in North America, project and policy evaluation relied solely on cost-benefit analysis. If, for example, the benefits of building a reservoir could be shown to outweigh the construction costs, project approval was generally given. However, increased project and policy failures led legislators and policy makers to seek something other than narrow economic criteria for project and policy evaluation. Of particular interest was how new projects and sometimes the abandonment of older ones were impacting both the biophysical environment and human communities. Thus environmental, social, technological and health assessments—**the need to understand change in advance**—were born!

If you wish to begin your project
skip to **Chapter 4**, page 33

➡

The U.S. National Environmental Policy Act of 1969

The U.S. President, Richard Nixon, signed the National Environmental Policy Act of 1969 (NEPA) on January 1, 1970. Under that law, proponents of development projects and policies that involved U.S. federal land, federal tax dollars or federal jurisdictions were required to file an environmental impact statement (EIS) detailing the impacts of the proposal, as well as project alternatives, on the physical, cultural and human environments. The NEPA legislation also required <u>mitigation</u> measures for impacts and a <u>monitoring program</u> to ensure that <u>mitigation</u> was actually working (➡ NEPA, 1969). Very few members of Congress, the industrial development community, environmentalists, or indeed Nixon himself, foresaw how the new law would change the way the world community looked at environmental and social impacts of development. Henry "Scoop" Jackson, the Senator in 1969 from the U. S. State of Washington, was responsible for including the "triggering mechanism" in the NEPA legislation, which required an Environmental Impact Assessment (EIA) if federal land, laws or monies were involved. The inclusion of the triggering mechanism was a unique legislative requirement and ensured that an EIS would actually be done.

NEPA Legislation and the Trans-Alaska Pipeline Permit

"The three year environmental impact assessment of the proposed Trans-Alaska pipeline was the forerunner of the bio-physical content of the modern day EIS. Unfortunately, the need for social and economic impact assessment was only noted at the end of that permitting process."

Figure 2-1 shows a chronology of the key events in the history of impact assessment, particularly in North America. In February, 1970, the Bureau of Land Management in the U.S. Department of the Interior submitted a six-page EIS statement to accompany the application for the Trans-Alaska pipeline permit from Prudhoe Bay to Valdez, Alaska. Two days later the Wilderness Society, the Friends of the Earth and the Environmental Defense Fund filed suit contending that the EIS statement was inadequate because it did not consider, for example, the consequences to permafrost of pumping hot oil through a pipe laying on the ground. In addition, no provision was made for disruption to the annual migration of several caribou herds due to the pipeline and the road that was to be built beside it. Although not specifically mentioned in the litigation, some observers wondered where all those construction workers and their families would be housed who came north to work on the pipeline (➡ Dixon, 1978:3). Three years later the permit to build the pipeline was issued. In the meantime, the EIS had grown from six pages to six feet. More importantly, most of the potential environmental problems had been addressed to the satisfaction of the courts, the plaintiffs and the Alyeska Pipeline Company (a collection of U.S. and Canadian oil companies that owned leases on Prudhoe Bay). Anticipatory planning had worked and all sides agreed that the NEPA (National Environmental Policy Act) process had allowed project proponents to deal with issues that might otherwise have been overlooked. Until the Exxon Valdez set sail on Prince William Sound in March of 1989, no unforeseen environmental damage could be traced to pipeline activity.

Figure 2.1

Key Events in the History of Environmental and Social Impact Assessment

1969	Passage of the U.S. National Environmental Policy Act (NEPA) (signed first day of 1970)
1970	First World-Wide Earth Day—April 22nd
1970	Suit filed against Alyeska Pipeline Company and Department of the Interior over the EIS prepared for the permit allowing construction of the Trans-Alaska Pipeline in North America
1971-1976	Expansion of NEPA style legislation into 16 U.S. States
1970-1973	Initial attempts to prepare EIAs by the U.S. Army Corps of Engineers
1970-1976	Courts clarify the requirements of Environmental Impact Assessment (EIA)
1973	Council on Environmental Quality (CEQ) issues draft guidelines for the preparation of environmental impact statements
1973	Environmental Assessment and Review Process (EARP) established in Canada (amended in 1977 and formalized in the Canadian Environmental Assessment Act of 1992)
1974	Beginning of Chief Justice Berger (British Columbia, Canada Supreme Court) inquiry regarding the proposed Mackenzie Valley Pipeline from the Beaufort Sea to Edmonton
1974	EDRA-1 Environmental Design Research Associates meet in Milwaukee, Wisconsin-first academic/professional meeting on SIA
1978	Final CEQ guidelines for preparation of EIA statements
1980	*Environmental Impact Assessment Review*—first issue published
1981	International Association for Impact Assessment (IAIA) founded in Toronto at the 1981 meeting of the American Association for the Advancement of Science (AAAS)
1982	First International Social Impact Assessment Conference in Vancouver, B.C., Canada.
1983	Most U.S. land agencies adopt regulations for environmental and social assessment
1986	CEQ issues updated EIA regulations
1986	World Bank requires environmental impact assessment for all funded projects (most regional banks follow)
1987	*Our Common Future* (the Brundtland Commission report published)
1989	European Economic Community requires environmental impact assessment
1992	Earth Summit in Rio de Janeiro, Brazil (sustainability integrated into SIA-EIA)
1993	U.S. Council on Environmental Quality considers Social Impact Assessment Guidelines and Principles in EIA procedures
1994	Environmental Assessment Summit in Quebec City, Canada
1996	UN Environmental Programme (UNEP) issues EIA "Best Practices"
1999	World Bank circulates draft guidelines for SIA (later rescinded)
2000	European community (ECC) issues draft SIA guidelines
2001	UNDP funds the integration of SIA and EIA procedures in selected countries
2003	Revised and updated *U.S. Principles and Guidelines for SIA* published by the U.S. Inter Organizational Committee on Principles and Guidelines
2004	*International Principles for Social Impact Assessment* published by IAIA
2007	Canadian Aboriginal populations require SIA for resource extraction permits

Who First Used the Term Social Impact Assessment?

After the permit to build the Trans-Alaska pipeline was issued, one of the Inuit Chiefs made this comment "...now that we have dealt with the problem of the permafrost and the caribou and what to do with hot oil, what about changes in the customs and ways of my people?...(Dixon, 1978:4)." Unfortunately, as the Inuit chief pointed out, the social impacts on both the indigenous and other Alaskan peoples were never addressed. Would the traditional cultures and way of life be changed by so massive of a construction project? What about the influx of construction workers who spoke different dialectics (of English) and brought with them a distinctive life style? Obviously, with a total population of 351,000 (in 1973) the State of Alaska could provide only a fraction of the estimated 42,000 persons that would work on the pipeline during the periods of peak construction. Because of these and other related events the impacts of development on the human populations began to be discussed alongside bio-physical and economic alterations (Dixon, 1978:8). The term social impact assessment (SIA) was first used in 1973 to refer to potential changes in the indigenous Inuit Alaskan culture due to pipeline construction.

Mackenzie Valley Gas Pipeline Inquiry

One of the key events in establishing the importance of social impact assessment in project appraisal was the Mackenzie Valley pipeline inquiry. Between 1974 and 1978, Justice T.R. Berger of the British Columbia (Canada) Supreme Court, conducted an extensive inquiry into a proposed pipeline from Mackenzie Bay in the Beaufort Sea along the Richardson Mountains with connections to pipelines in British Columbia and Alberta (Gamble, 1978 and Berger, 1983). Although proposed by Canadian oil companies, the money to build it came from the U.S., because the natural gas and oil would end up in the Chicago market. The case represents the first time that the social effects of a development on Aboriginal populations were considered in depth. An extensive public consultation was implemented, in which native populations were provided funding to hold public hearings and present their views in their local dialect. As a result of the findings of this inquiry, the permit for construction was denied. The Mackenzie Valley pipeline is the first case where the decision not to proceed was based on social impacts (Gamble, 1978; Berger, 1983).

U.S. Council on Environmental Quality (CEQ) issues Guidelines for Environmental Impact Assessment

The U.S. Council on Environmental Quality (CEQ) published preliminary guidelines for doing an environmental impact statement in 1973, formalized them in 1978 and provided a detailed update in 1986. The spirit and intent of the NEPA legislation is captured in the following outline.

1. ***Description of Proposed Actions*** The description of the project or proposed policy change must be presented in enough depth that a reader might visualize the project or the policy change. The guidelines further stipulated that only well thought-out proposals should be considered.

2. ***Relationship of the Proposed Action to Land Use Plans*** Because land development and alteration is part of many projects, the EIS statement must specify how the land and its present use will be altered. In many cases, this section deals with changes in zoning regulations. For example, housing projects might change the population density of residential areas or forest lands might be converted from timber production to recreational areas.

3. ***Probable Impact on the Environment*** In this section, the project proponents must detail how the proposed action will alter the existing "environment." In the initial legislation the terms "cultural, physical, historical and social" were used to define the environment. However, most early environmental impact statements were restricted to assessments of biological and physical alteration and changes in natural resource use.

4. ***Alternatives to the Proposed Actions*** The spirit of the NEPA regulations is that for every proposed action and policy there may be an alternative that would accomplish the same objective with less disruption to the human and physical environment. For example, instead of building an expensive nuclear power plant, the same objective could be accomplished by a combination of smaller generators powered by natural gas coupled with education, financial incentives for energy conservation and solar panels.

> "The NEPA process has become a generic term for doing environmental and social impact assessment as a way of considering alternatives to project proposals."

5. ***Unavoidable Adverse Effects*** The very process of development brings about alteration in the human and physical environment. Many changes are unavoidable and are referred to as the consequences of development. The NEPA legislation required that any adverse effects be detailed, understood, and <u>mitigation</u> procedures be implemented (Chapter 13 in this book).

6. ***Local Short-term Versus Long-term Social Impacts*** The environmental and social impact assessment must differentiate between short-term impacts that are project related and presumably will go away and enduring long-term impacts. During reservoir construction the influx of construction workers and materials causes severe short-term disruption in the local community. The primary impacts, however, may be more severe, i.e., an influx of weekend visitors, on-going maintenance and financing of community infrastructure or the loss of family/living wage jobs as workers leave.

7. ***Irreversible and Irretrievable Impacts*** The EIS-SIA statement must specify those consequences to the human population and the environment that will be forever changed. The damming of a wild and scenic river means that the resource is lost forever. Highway and reservoir construction alters the lives

of individuals and families who must relocate and could split existing communities.

8. ***Other Considerations*** The EIS statement must include additional and "unusual" environmental and social impacts that may not be easily specified or categorized. For example, the psychological impact of living near a nuclear power plant may not be easily quantified but persons may perceive its operation a real threat to their health and safety.

Canada: Environmental Assessment and Review Process (EARP)

In 1973, a Canadian Federal Cabinet Directive established a process for environmental assessment involving federal activity. The policy initiative was updated and amended in 1977. In 1984 the Environmental Assessment and Review Process (EARP) Guidelines Order were issued. A 1989 Federal Court decision stated that the EARP Guidelines Order was a regulation binding on the Crown and, therefore, enforceable by the courts. Following the court decision Parliament began to develop a Federal Environmental Assessment Act. The outcome was the passage, in 1992, of the Canadian Environmental Assessment Act (CEAA). CEAA is now the basis for Canadian Federal EA and, since 1995, has replaced the EARP Guidelines Order.

The term ***environment*** in the CEAA legislation is defined in biophysical terms with no reference to socio-economic components. However, the Act requires a consideration of a project's environmental effects and includes reference to an effect of a change to the environment (as defined in biophysical terms) on "health and socio-economic conditions". In practice what this means is that there is only a legal requirement to examine impacts on health and social and economic conditions if these impacts are a by-product of an impact in the natural environment.

Some Canadian Provincial EA processes require a direct assessment of socio-economic impacts. It is partly because social and economic impacts tend to be more of an area of Provincial responsibility, in that CEAA only has an oblique reference to the consideration of social and economic impacts.

The Spread of SIA outside North America

By the 1980s many developed countries as well as international donor/lending organizations had adopted or were considering SIA as part of their EIA requirements in national legislation or agency policy (📖 *Concepts*, Chapter 12). Developers in both the private and public sector recognized the benefits of SIA and EIA. Even in the more development oriented ministries and agencies, there was recognition that SIA actually improved project implementation and success rates. This attitude change is due in large part to project failures resulting from inadequate appraisal based on narrow economic and technical criteria.

In 1985, the European Economic Community (EEC) began to recommend environmental impact statements for their members and by 1989 the recommendation became a requirement. The event is significant, not only because of the diversity of language and cultures involved, but the recognition that biophysical and social impacts due to environment alteration do not stop at national boundaries.

An equally important event happened in 1986 when the World Bank made a public commitment to include environmental impact assessment in their appraisal process. The event was important because the requirement represented a split with the Reagan Administration policy of minimizing environmental assessment. By the late 80s it was obvious that many World Bank funded projects were failing due to environmental problems and a lack of fit with the social and cultural milieu of the targeted communities. Taking their cue from the World Bank, regional banks and bi-lateral aid agencies began to incorporate environmental and social impact assessment into their project appraisal procedures.

The decision of the World Bank was further reinforced by publication in 1987 of *Our Common Future*, by the United Nations Committee on Environment and Development (UNCED). Commonly known as the *Brundtland Report*, the recommendations on sustainability received wide acceptance outside of North America and accelerated worldwide interest in environmental and social impact assessment. The need for impact assessment was enhanced by a continued string of environmental disasters due primarily to the lack of prior planning. Decision-makers within many governments and bi-lateral aid, lending and donor agencies were turning away from narrow cost-benefit analysis in project evaluation and instead opting for an emphasis on long-run ecosystem sustainability. Social and environmental impact assessment and strategic environmental assessment (SEA) (⌷ *Concepts*, Chapter 10) provided the framework with which to conduct such evaluations.

The International Association for Impact Assessment

The founding of the International Association for Impact Assessment (IAIA) in 1981 provided an international forum for persons interested in research and the practice of EIS, SIA, technological assessment and other types of project appraisal methodologies. A year later, IAIA began publishing a journal titled *Impact Assessment Bulletin (now Impact Assessment and Project Appraisal)*, which provided an outlet for academics and practitioners to publish research and practice in the many sub-fields of impact assessment.

IAIA has over 500 international members representing 100 different counties plus individual chapter affiliates in such diverse locations as South Africa, Beijing, Cameroon, Ghana, Chile, Nigeria, Senegal as well as three in Canada and one in the Washington D.C. area of the U.S. The Association promotes good assessment practice and lobbies national governments, NGOs, bi-lateral aid and donor agencies to incorporate environmental assessment and sustainability practices in their appraisal procedures (www.iaia.org).

Important Benefits of EIA-SIA Legislation

The 70s and 80s were the decades in which the largest numbers of EIA statements were completed in the U.S. and Canada. By the end of that period, general agreement had been reached on the content of the EIA-SIA statements, and decision-makers, planners and the general public was beginning to reap the benefits of the NEPA process.

1. Doing environmental and social assessment changed policy makers thinking about the benefits of pre-planning (although in some cases only a little bit). The change was particularly true for project engineers and planners from a technical background who had witnessed project failure on non-technical grounds.

> "…a major benefit of EIA-SIA legislations is that many bad projects never get to the drawing board.:

2. As environmental planning before the decision became more accepted, officials in more development-oriented agencies and ministries saw the process as stopping or slowing economic development. However, the string of environmental disasters resulting from decisions made on narrow technical and economic data reinforced the need for environmental and social assessment in the very early stages of the planning process.

3. The NEPA process initiated a more general movement to examine other development and policy settings on an ex-ante basis. Knowledge gained in a variety of development settings made it possible to better understand future development events by looking at past events. Research by applied anthropologists, rural sociologists, psychologists and cultural geographers was becoming a factor in increasing the success rate of planned change.

4. Research on the types and frequency of exposure risks has made health effects an important part of the assessment process. Encouraged by members of the World Health Organization (WHO), health impact assessment (HIA) has now become a formalized part of IAIA.

5. Social and environmental impact assessment has permanently altered the way we look at and think about project planning, the appraisal process and development in general. The key to the NEPA legislation was anticipating change, be it the biophysical or human environment. The major benefit was that many bad projects were never proposed or at least were subjected to intense scrutiny. The NEPA legislation required that the consequences of the development on the human and biophysical environment be considered as part of the planning process.

Integrating EIA-SIA into the Planning Process

Initial failures to include environmental assessment in the planning process were classic cases of *who's to blame*. The *Impact Assessment Bulletin* (☛1990) of the International Association for Impact Assessment and *Environmental Impact Assessment Review* (☛1990) each devoted two issues to analyzing the problem and providing solutions for integrating EIA and SIA into the planning process.

1. The first problem, which by now is being overcome, is that early EIS and SIA statements were seldom prepared by planners or those trained in the planning process. Because EIAs were completed by the proponent and initially dealt with big construction projects, engineering and architectural consulting firms were the first "environmental assessors."

> "It is always easier to make a decision if you know in advance something about the consequences."

2. However, the engineers were not the only unprepared profession; urban and regional planners systematically ignored environmental and social issues in the planning process. Trained in land use allocation and layout, the planning profession had little experience in incorporating environmental and social concerns, as well as sustainability issues into the planning process. Furthermore, planning tended to be top-down and the affected population was seldom asked for input.

3. Outside of North America, the British Towne Planning System was the model for land use allocation and preservation. As part of the process, public comment was allowed before the final decision. However, the British approach did not specifically include an environmental component. The integration of EIA-SIA into the planning process was initially slowed because many countries using the British planning system assumed that environmental concerns would be accounted for through that process. However, by 2003, strategic environmental assessment, with a focus on sustainability, became part of English Structure Plans. Social and cultural components are included in those assessments (📖*Concepts*, Chapter 10).

4. However, if the goal of integrating EIA-SIA into the planning process is achieved, another planning dilemma emerges. Who is responsible for developing the mitigation plan and who is responsible for implementing a long-term monitoring program (Chapter 13 in this book)?

Now that you have read through Chapter 2, answer the following questions about the history of environmental and social impact assessment.

1. Name the piece of legislation which started the field of social and environmental impact assessment.

_____

2. What major event in the United States determined the content of EIA statements as we know them today?

_____

3. Name the project that after a series of public inquires established the need for social impact assessment among Aboriginal (indigenous) populations?

_____

4. The EIA-SIA process is similar to what other type of decision making?

_____

5. How can citizens benefit from participation in the SIA process? _____

_____

Now that we have reviewed the history of social impact assessment let's go on to **Chapter 3** where we learn more about the concepts and steps of the SIA process!

➡

If you are not interested in the concepts and theories of SIA go on to **Chapter 4**.

➡

Chapter 3. A Social Impact Assessment Model

> *Elected officials, local community leaders, and urban and regional planners must approve or disapprove proposals for public and private development projects as well as changes in local, provincial, and federal government programs and policies. These people need a better way to anticipate the possible social consequences of proposed actions on human populations and communities. Social impact assessment (SIA) offers an effective means of anticipating and planning for social impacts prior to project development or policy implementation.....Rabel J. Burdge, 1969*

Purpose of this chapter is to:

- Understand the comparative model of social impact assessment;
- Learn about the stages and steps in the social impact assessment process;
- Review a list of project types and policy settings which affect local communities;
- Learn about the selection of Social Impact Assessment (SIA) variables;
- Explore the relationship between social impact assessment and the planning process.

If you wish to skip background discussion and begin your project, turn to **Chapter 4** on page 33

A Conceptual Background to Social Impact Assessment

The social impact assessment model presented here combines an anthropological perspective with sociological, anthropological and social-psychological research on community level change resulting from project development and policy change. The sources of data are social science concepts and variables, shown by previous research to be related to attitudes and receptivity toward development activity as well as quality-of-life measures obtained from a variety of information sources.

The approach to social impact assessment is practical rather than theoretical. In seeking to understand the behavior of people and communities affected by social change, we hope to predict the probable impacts of development and policy change. Using a comparative model, we study the course of events in a community where planned change has occurred and extrapolate from that analysis what is likely to happen in another community where a similar developmental event is planned. Put another way, we wish to know if given similar pre-development conditions and similar development projects, can the social impacts resulting from a similar event in Community A be generalized to and help us understand what will happen in Community B?

Another goal of predicting social impacts is humanistic and based on the intent of the initial U. S. NEPA legislation. We want to identify irreversible and undesirable social effects before they occur in order that recommendations for mediation may be made based on research. It is the planning agency, the project proponent or the appropriate federal, state, provincial or municipality, as well as the local community which must develop and coordinate mitigation efforts. The SIA model also allows us to think about possible alternative ways to achieve the same objectives of a proposed action. Moreover, if social impacts can be measured and understood, recommendations for mitigating actions on the part of both the proponent and the community can be made. In Chapter 13 we outline a procedure for mitigation/enhancement of project and policy change.

It is almost impossible to catalogue all dimensions of social impacts; because change has a way of creating other changes, much as the proverbial rock thrown in a pond—complexity increases with each ring. However, social scientists have identified and are able to measure the fundamental social components of a community. Studied over time, dimensions such as changing power structures, migration patterns and community cohesion provide insight as to how community social structure and organization will be altered when planned and unplanned change occurs. Faced with a proposal to build a new hospital, close a factory or expand a park—community leaders, planners as well as the private or public sector organizations proposing the change can learn from the experience of other communities that have undergone similar types of change.

> "History tells us that the best way to learn about the future is to look at past events. Will individual and community response to change be the same given similar events?"

The Basic Social Impact Assessment Strategy

The objective of the SIA process is to anticipate and predict social impacts in advance so that the findings and recommendations may become part of the planning and decision making process.

The model illustrated in Figure 3.1 depicts the approach utilized in uncovering the major social impacts of proposed development projects. The social assessor first identifies similar projects that are on-going and attempts to locate the impacts resulting from the planned change (the comparative study). Ideally, information about the community or area of study would be available both before and after the event to help in measurement. Social impacts then become the changes taking place between T_{1a} and T_{2a} (comparative study (**a**)).The impact study (**b**) attempts to predict the change between T_{2b} and T_{3b} based on the research and information accumulated from comparative studies of similar social impact settings. If available, a control study (**c**) where no event took place would help demonstrate the on-going effects of social change (the difference between T_{1c}, T_{2c} and T_{3c}).

Figure 3.1
The Basic Social Impact Assessment Model

Comparative Study (**a**) $T_{1a}\text{---------}\overset{\mathbf{X_a}}{\text{------}}>T_{2a}$ **X**=Development

Impact study (b) $T_{2b}\text{-----}\overset{\mathbf{X_b}}{\text{---------}}>T_{3b}$

Control study (c) $T_{1c}\text{---------------}>T_{2c}\text{---------------}>T_{3c}\text{------------------}>T_{4c}$
                        (Past)   (Present)   (Future)   (Far Future)

Therefore, the basic SIA strategy becomes one of identifying likely future social impacts based on reconstructing the social impacts of past events. The basic SIA model (Fig. 3.1) may be thought of as a series of snapshots taken at different intervals. Missing information is then filled in based on data obtained from an extensive literature review.

Another strength of the SIA model shown in Figure 3.1 is that with appropriate data sources (those which can be collected frequently such as land transfer records and employment levels), it allows for a dynamic interpretation of events and can provide monitoring of short-term impacts. Monitoring provides a continual source of evaluation or check on the type and direction of predictions made about social impacts.

Stages in Project/Policy Development

All projects and policies go through a series of stages, starting with initial planning; next implementation and/or construction, and carrying through to operation and maintenance (see Figure 3.2). At some point the project might be abandoned or decommissioned, or official policy could change. Social impacts will be different at each stage. Scoping (Chapter 4) of issues may lead the social assessor to focus only on one stage. For example, one community might be concerned about public response to the proposed siting of a hazardous waste disposal facility; another with the construction aspects of pipelines; and a third might be faced with a change in the designation of public land from timber production to recreational use. The specific stage in life of the project or policy is an important factor in determining effects. Remember, not all social impacts will occur at each stage. Figure 3.2 illustrates the stages in project/policy development.

Figure 3.2
Stages in Project/Policy Development

| Stage 1. Planning/policy development |
| Stage 2. Construction/implementation |
| Stage 3. Operation/maintenance |
| Stage 4. Decommissioning/abandonment |

Planning/Policy Development refers to all activity that takes place from the time a project or policy is proposed to the point of construction activity or policy implementation. Examples include project design, revision, public comment, licensing, the evaluation of alternatives, and the decision to go ahead. Social impacts actually begin the day a proposed action is announced and can be measured from that point.

> "Change begins to take place the instant a new policy change or project or a closure is announced."

Many community leaders and policy makers often assume that no social impacts will take place until, for example, construction starts, or recreational fees are charged on public land or zoning laws are changed to allow for increased housing density. However, real, measurable, and often significant effects on the *human environment* begin to take place as soon as there are changes in *social or economic* conditions. From the time of the earliest announcement of a pending policy change or rumors about a project, both hopes and hostilities can begin to mount; speculators can lock up potentially important properties; politicians can maneuver for benefits; and interest groups often form to support or reject a proposal. These changes occur by simply introducing information about the proposed action into a community.

Construction/Implementation The construction/implementation stage begins when a decision is made to proceed, a permit is issued or a law or regulation is implemented. Typical construction projects involve clearing land, building access roads, developing utilities and so forth. Displacement and relocation of people, as necessary, occurs during this phase. Depending on the scale of the project, the buildup of a migrant construction work force may take place. If significant in-migration occurs, new residents may require an expanded community infrastructure. Communities may have difficulties in meeting the need for schools, health facilities, housing and other social services. Mental stress may be created by changing patterns of social interaction, conflict between newcomers and long-time residents, by sudden increases in the cost of housing and local services, and even by increased uncertainty about the future. When new policies are implemented, local economies and organizations may change, and old behaviors are replaced with new ways of interaction among community members and even in the use of public and private property.

Operation/Maintenance The operation/maintenance stage occurs after the construction is complete or the policy is fully operational. In many cases, this stage will require fewer workers, as in pipeline maintenance, than the construction/implementation phase. If operations continue at a relatively stable level for an extended period, changes during this stage can often be the most beneficial. Communities seeking industrial development will often focus on this stage due to stable high wage employment or the benefits from increased property and sales tax. It is during this stage that the communities can adapt to new social and economic conditions; accommodation can take place and the expectations of positive effects—such as stable population, a quality infrastructure and enhanced leisure opportunities—can be realized.

> "Closure may have positive benefits–for example, downstream water quality might improve if a polluting industry was actually forced to close down."

Abandonment/Decommissioning begins when the proposal (or decision) is made that the project or policy and associated activity will cease at some time in the future. As in the planning stage, the social impacts of decommissioning begin when the intent to close down is announced and the community or region must adapt; but this time to the loss of the project or an adjustment to a policy change. Closure sometimes means the loss of the economic base, as for example a manufacturing facility or the closing of a distribution center. At other times, the disruption to the local community may be lessened or at least altered if one type of employment is replaced by another, as in the case of the Hanford Facility in the U.S. State of Washington where nuclear production facilities were closed down, but employment actually increased as environmental cleanup specialists were hired to help clean up nuclear contamination at the facility. In other cases, disruption may be exacerbated if the community is not only losing its present economic base, but has lost the capacity to return to a former economic base. Morgan City, Louisiana which had been the self proclaimed "shrimp capital of the world" in the 1950s is a good example of a community that lost its capacity to return to a former economic base. During the 1960s and 1970s the employment in this community shifted to offshore oil development. When oil prices collapsed in the 1980s, the community found it could not return to the shrimp industry because shrimp-processing facilities had closed down and most of the shrimp boats had been allowed to decay or had moved to other fishing grounds. Ironically, those workers were again needed to clean-up the BP Deepwater Horizon oil spill of 2010.

Relating the Project Type and to the Project Setting

Projects and policy decisions that both require and benefit from social impact assessment range from prison and plant sitings, to highway, reservoir, and power plant construction, to managing old growth forests to maintaining a biologically diverse region. Accordingly, the setting for doing SIA may range from isolated wilderness areas to urban neighborhoods, each with special characteristics that affect social impacts. Social impacts (as well as economic and physical changes) will vary depending upon the type of project or policy setting. The following are examples of project types, settings, and policy changes requiring social and environmental impact assessment:

> "...the assessor should be mindful that social impacts will vary among project settings."

- Mineral extraction, including surface, ocean and underground mining as well as new oil and gas drilling to include "fracking" of shale deposits.
- Hazardous and sanitary waste sites, including the construction and operation of disposal sites for a variety of hazardous and sanitary wastes (also included are facilities that burn or otherwise destroy chemical and toxic wastes).
- Power plants, including both nuclear and fossil fuel electrical generating facilities and associated developments.
- Reservoirs, including all water impoundments for flood control, hydropower, conservation, and recreation; and cooling lakes and diversion structures as well as irrigation projects.
- Industrial plants (manufacturing facilities generally built and operated by the private sector, e.g., refineries, steel mills, assembly lines).
- Land use designations, e.g., a change from timber production to wilderness designation, from private property to public parkland.
- Military and governmental installations, including base closures and openings.
- Schools, public and private, including primary, secondary, and university.
- Transportation facilities, including airports, streets, terminals.
- Linear developments, including subways, railroads, power lines, aqueducts, irrigation canals, bike paths, bridges, pipelines, sewers, fences, walls and barrier channels, green belts, and waterways.
- Trade facilities, including businesses and shopping centers.
- Designation of sacred, historical, archeological and cultural sites.
- Parks and preserves, refuges, cemeteries, and recreation areas.
- Housing facilities, including apartments, office buildings, and hospitals.
- Prisons and other detention facilities.
- Municipal, state, provincial and federal zoning land use policies.

Identifying the Social Impact Assessment Variables

SIA variables point to measurable change in human populations, communities, and social relationships resulting from a development project or policy change. Drawing upon research on local community change, rural industrialization, reservoir and highway development, natural resource development, and social change in general, I have delineated a list of 28 social variables under the general headings of **population impacts, community/institutional arrangements, communities in transition, individual and family level impacts, and community infrastructure needs** (Fig. 3.3).

How Did I Select a Social Impact Variable?

The 28 SIA variables shown in Figure 3.3 represent the types of social impacts arising from planned change in both rural and urban communities. Research continues on the list of SIA variables as well as methods to measure each in advance of the proposed action. Chapters 7-11 in this book demonstrate a measure for each of these variables and how the measurement might be applied and interpreted in the social assessment process. The following criteria were used in selecting and developing the current 28 SIA variables shown in Figure 3.3.

An SIA variable helps us understand how a community may be altered by project development and policy change. SIA variables do not refer to the total social environment; they explain only the consequences of the proposed impact event. Other portions of an environmental assessment or planning document cover financial, biophysical and land use changes.

An SIA variable will tell the decision-maker, proponent or planner a specific consequence of the proposed action. Such descriptors as increase, decrease, expand or contract, depend upon the type of project as well as the geographical and political setting. The directionality of change is not assumed in the labeling of SIA variables.

An SIA variable must have a discrete, nominal, or continuous empirical indicator that can be measured, collected, and interpreted within the context of a specific social impact setting.

All SIA variables are based upon data that can be collected or made available during the planning and decision stage as well as other stages in the development of the project or policy (Figure. 3.2). Because SIA information is required before a decision is made, I rely upon data that can be collected and analyzed in advance of the decision regarding the proposed action.

Figure 3.3
Social Impact Assessment Variables:
The Current List of Twenty Eight

Population Impacts

1. Population change
2. Influx or out flux of temporary workers
3. Presence of seasonal (leisure) residents
4. Relocation of individuals and families
5. Dissimilarity in age, gender, racial or ethnic composition

Community/Institutional Arrangements

6. Formation of attitudes toward the project
7. Interest group activity
8. Alteration in size and structure of local government
9. Presence of planning and zoning activity
10. Industrial diversification
11. Living/Family Wage
12. Enhanced economic inequities
13. Change in employment equity of minority groups
14. Change in occupational opportunities

Communities in Transition

15. Presence of an outside agency
16. Inter-organizational cooperation
17. Introduction of new social classes
18. Change in the commercial/industrial focus of the area
19. Presence of weekend residents (recreational)

Individual and Family Level Impacts

20. Disruption in daily living and movement patterns
21. Dissimilarity in religious and cultural practices
22. Alteration in family structure
23. Disruption in social networks
24. Perceptions of public health and safety
25. Change in leisure opportunities

Community Infrastructure Needs

26. Change in community infrastructure
27. Land acquisition and disposal
28. Effects on known cultural, historical, sacred and archaeological resources

An SIA variable does not require, but may utilize, information from surveys of the general population. Survey data vary in quality depending upon the amount of care taken in questionnaire design, sampling, and in the training of interviewers. Most community and project level assessors have neither the time nor the expertise to do detailed survey research. However, data from well designed questionnaires–addressed to limited objectives-always enhance the understanding of community response to planned social change. A few countries forbid questionnaire studies of the general population.

An SIA variable is not to be confused with such sociological labels as middle class, ethnicity, or small groups. These labels define sociological concepts and situations but do not describe changes that take place in communities due to project development. The name of each SIA variable was chosen to minimize the use of social science (sociological) jargon.

Figure 3.4
Social Impact Assessment Variables by Project Setting and Project Stage—an Example

Project Settings	Project Stage			
	Planning/Policy	Construction/ Implementation	Operation/ Maintenance	Decommission/ Abandonment
Hazardous Waste Site	Perceptions of public health and safety	Influx of temporary workers	Relocation of families	Alteration in size of local government
Industrial Plant	Formation of attitudes toward the project	Change in community infrastructure	Change in the industrial focus of the community	Change in employment equity of minority groups

Figure 3.4 provides an abbreviated matrix of how the SIA variables (as listed in Fig. 3.3) might apply within the context of both the setting and the stage of a project. The first example is the siting of a hazardous waste facility. Perceptions about problems of public health and safety could emerge during the planning stage. If the project is approved, construction would be accompanied by an influx of temporary workers. In the case of the industrial plant, an expanded community infrastructure might be needed during both construction and operation, while a change in the industrial focus of the community might occur during the operation stage. These analytical procedures are repeated for each of the SIA variables for each stage of the project. In short, the SIA process allows the user to identify and understand the SIA variables that apply to each stage of the project under consideration. Figure 3.4 further illustrates how the SIA variables become part of the Social Impact Assessment (SIA) and therefore a major source of information for planners and decision-makers.

Steps in the Social Impact Assessment Process

Figure 3.5. outlines the basic steps for analyzing social impacts of a project or a policy change. Each step corresponds (approximately) to a chapter in this book (*A Community Guide to Social Impact Assessment*). After you have read through the basic steps in the Social Impact Assessment process, compare them with the steps in the planning process as shown in 📖 *Concepts*, Chapters 3, 7 and 22.

Figure 3.5. Basic Steps in the Social Impact Assessment (SIA) Process

1. **Develop Public Involvement Program:** At this stage the social assessor must develop a public involvement program to guide the selection of stakeholders and detail the procedures for including interested citizens in the decision process, 📖 *Concepts* pp 215-244.

2. **Describe the Proposed Action (and possible alternatives)**: In the next step develop a clear statement as to the proposed action in consultation with the proponent and its likely area of impact and community boundaries. Remember technical and policy details (Chapter 4).

3. **History and Baseline Conditions (The Social Profile):** Describe the proposed action in the context of historical and present baseline human/environmental conditions in the community or region (Chapter 4).

4. **Scoping**: Begin to identify the full range of social impacts that will be addressed based on interviews/discussion with all stakeholders, the proponents and based on a thorough review of the literature and previous studies (Chapters 4 and 5). A stand alone SIA may require a peer review of the scope of your SIA work plan.

5. **Investigate/Understand Effects of the Proposed Action**: Gather detailed data for each social impact assessment variable identified during Scoping and by Stakeholders using a variety of investigative and analytical strategies and data sources (Chapters 7-11).

6. **Projecting Response to Project/Policy Effects (Determine Significance)**: This step requires determining and interpreting identified significant impacts revealed in the detailed SIA analysis (Chapters 6 and 12).

7. **Changes in Proposed Action/Alternatives:** Based on the social impact assessment, a decision on the proposed project or policy will be made or recommended. Alternatives may be considered, in which case additional social assessments may be needed.

8. **Mitigation\Enhancement Activity**: Based on significant social impacts identified during the analysis, develop a variety of mitigation measures to minimize negative impacts and maximize possible benefits (Chapter 13).

9. **Monitoring and Social Follow-ups**: Utilizing data from each of the significant social impacts, implement a monitoring procedure to involve both the proponent and the community. (Chapter 13). Social follow-ups or ex-post facto analysis will help in understanding if what was predicted actually happened. An IBA could now me in place to include enforcement procedures Some Adaptive Management may be required at this point.

How Does Social Impact Assessment Fit the Planning Process?

SIA may be used as a planning or policy tool in the decision making process.

1. *Planning Tool* Planning can be divided into three main stages: *policy* (which defines broad, socially desired goals and outlines the means to obtain them); *programs* (which put into operation the means and channels resources toward satisfying ends) and *projects* (which represent the actual implementation of activities designed to further the goals established in policy and programs).

> "SIA is especially necessary in these areas to facilitate forecasting of social impacts, because planning for change before it occurs rather than reacting to change after it occurs is a major purpose of SIA. In essence, SIA supports judgment with analysis." (Michaelson, 1976:8)

2. *Policy Tool* Policy selection entails two decisions: to act and to decide between alternatives in relation to some predefined goal or objective. By providing a balanced appraisal of alternative courses of action, SIA can become a tool to enhance the selection process from a range of policy options. In a sense SIA helps make policy by evaluating alternatives.

3. *Decision Making Tool* As a decision making tool, SIA is a part of the *rational problem solving process* serving to facilitate decision making activities by determining the range of *social costs* and *social benefits* of the proposed and alternative courses of action. The decision making process is often filled with conflict. As we learned in Chapter 1, the different actors in the SIA process hold different values and interests and interact differently in pursuit of different goals. SIA helps to reduce conflict and enable a more rational decision because the SIA statement provides data on most of the issues and alternatives. The original U.S. NEPA legislation includes the action forcing or "triggering" provision. Each project or policy that affects federal land, funds or legislation is required to prepare an EIS statement.

If Social Impact Assessment is all that great—why isn't everybody doing it?

1. Social impact assessment developed along with environmental impact assessment during the early 1970s as a methodological tool with which to better understand the consequences of environmental alteration and as an input to environmental impact statements. Unfortunately, social impacts have not always been included within an EIS statement.

2. For the most part, the assessment of biophysical and economic impacts has become a required input in the planning process. However, social impacts are not always arrayed alongside economic, biological, and land use changes in the matrix that leads to the final decision.

3. The major difficulty in the application of SIA process has been identifying and measuring the social impacts that occur in different development settings. Even when important social impacts are identified, few qualitative and quantitative indicators have been developed for measuring them.

4. When either social costs or benefits to local communities are arrayed against regional and national economic goals, social concerns generally finish a distant second. ***Social and environmental costs are almost always borne at the local level and these same communities must deal with the consequences.***

5. Social science research has yet to establish that the effects on human populations alone are significant enough to alter the outcome of the decision process. However, it is becoming obvious that project success is increasingly dependent upon *the principal of free prior and informed consent.*

Review of Chapter Three

1. The strategy behind the basic social impact assessment model is _____

    _____as borrowed from anthropology by Burdge and Johnson.

2. The name of the U.S. Senator considered by most to be the "father" of the NEPA

    legislation is _____.

3. The _____is a research tool used by both ecologists and sociologists to organize their analysis during the assessment process.

4. Which of the following is **not** a stage of project/policy development?

a. Construction/implementation
b. Planning/policy development
c. Public involvement
d. Abandonment/closure
e. Operation/maintenance

5. Major uses of social impact assessment are:

a. To help citizens understand the consequences of project development.
b. To uncover alternatives in achieving project/policy goals.
c. To understand impacts and change in advance of the event.
d. To maximize the benefits and minimize the costs of social change.
e. All of the above.

6. **T   or   F**   Social impacts begin with the announcement of a proposed project or policy change and can be measured from that point.

On to Chapter 4 to begin the Social Impact Assessment for your project.

Chapter 4. Getting Started—Identifying the Proposed Action: Scoping-Part I

To prepare this manual, on *A Community Guide to Social Impact Assessment*, we asked interested citizens, community leaders and professional change agents both in North America and internationally to identify the most common development events and policy issues facing the communities where they worked. The following activities stood out: closing and siting of waste facilities; park and expansion of facilities for tourists; highway corridors and transportation facilities; timber cutting and mineral extraction; agricultural and irrigation projects; consolidation of local government units; the closing of businesses and industrial plants; siting energy development facilities; adding major retail services; the listing of endangered species; dealing with urban sprawl; and the development of large residential/recreational housing complexes. Throughout this book, we will use examples from many of these *development projects and policy change settings* to illustrate specific social impact variables, but we will use four scenarios: siting of a waste facility, adding a major business, building a tourist destination facility and the closing of a rural hospital--to illustrate the practice of SIA. In training courses we also use the proposed Ajax Cooper and Gold Mine at the edge of Kamloops, British Columbia, Canada and the development of a housing and golf course in Central Queensland, Australia.

Chapters 4, 5 and 6 deal with the SIA Scoping Process. Chapter 4 will help you work through the first steps from describing the proposed action to determining the region or zone of influence to the identification of stakeholders. Chapter 5 will help you think about and identify possible social impacts. Chapter 6 introduces sources of information and a general overview of measurement procedures.

Steps in the Scoping Process

Describe the Proposed Action → Do a Social Profile → Determine Stage in the Development Process → Identification of Stake Holders → Determine Region or Zone of Influence → Identify Potential Social Impacts → Methods and Measurements → Be Aware of Possible Alternatives → Develop Plan of Work.

Let's set the stage!

➡

Four SIA Scenarios: Case Studies for Application

Case 1. Siting a Solid Waste Facility

Acme Waste Management is a large corporation organized to collect and dispose of a variety of hazardous and conventional industrial and household waste. Their landfills are running out of space and within two years many will close. **Acme** is seeking waste disposal facilities sites along interstate highways within 100 miles of Terre Haute, St Louis and Chicago in the central U.S. They have taken options on farms of at least 300 acres in many rural Illinois, Indiana, Iowa and Missouri communities with the goal of obtaining permits to build new waste facilities. **Acme** has chosen a 450 acre site in west central Illinois near the town of Arvana. The area is classified as agricultural. Depending upon the location, the final permit will be issued by a Village or Municipal Council or the elected County Commissioners. Local leaders are asking if they want such a facility and what will be citizen reaction. They want to know if it will alter the "way of life" in their community. How can they be sure that the many benefits promised by Acme will really be delivered?

Case 2. Adding a Major Business

Barn-Wall is an international retailer which specializes in building discount department stores on the edge of small rural communities where parking is plentiful and access is easy. **Barn-Wall** has chosen several rural counties as possible sites and has taken options on land near highway interchanges. The developers also propose to include space in the "**Barn-Wall Shopping Center**" for small retail outlets and fast food restaurants. Darnell, a modest sized community along the interstate highway in the southern part of Clinton County, has been selected as one of the sites. While some members of the community appear to welcome the **Barn-Wall** store, others are not so sure. They wonder if it will force downtown merchants to close; many of whom are struggling to stay open. Students at the nearby college have been asked to do a social assessment of the changes that might take place if **Barn-Wall** locates in Darnell.

Case 3. Closing a Health Facility

The board of directors of **Crestview Hospital** has decided to close its doors after 60 years of service to the residents of Plainburg. This is a sad day for the community because residents will have to drive 72 miles to Regional City to obtain hospital and emergency medical care. This is a double blow, because not only was **Crestview** a big employer, but the professional staff and their families provided leadership for many community activities. Recently, several school districts in the county were forced to consolidate because of low enrollment, lack of funds and the "failure" to provide courses needed for university entrance. If that was not bad enough, the major manufacturing plant in the community burned three years ago and the owners chose not to rebuild, even though they were given many tax abatement incentives. Rural development coordinators have been asked to look at the proposed closing of **Crestview Hospital** to better understand the social consequences of all the combined closings and what, if anything, can be done to benefit from the situation and break the cycle of facility closings in Plainburg. The closing of the hospital is part of a larger trend to consolidate medical facilities in rural areas. The population of Plainburg is approximately 9,400.

Case 4. Building a Tourist Destination Facility

The **Canadian Dream Development Corporation** has proposed a 1,100 hectare recreational lake/residential development at Buchart in Island Municipality. When completed, the project would include a 300 hectare lake and 2,435 residential units made-up of 540 condominiums, 625 townhouses, and 1,270 single family residences with some on lots as large as one hectare. The development would also include 160 hectares of open space which would be used to construct a golf course and recreational facility and protect existing wetlands on the property. It is anticipated that this development would attract both permanent and seasonal residents from major communities within an eight-hour drive of the site. While this project would increase the tax base and the number of service jobs on Island Municipality, local citizens are concerned about how the project would alter the *way of life* of Butchart, a very quite community of only 4,500 residents. They are also concerned about the long intermittent construction period.

Activity 4.1 Focus on Projects and Policies in Your Community

Instructions: Now that you have examples of what might be happening in your community, let's focus on a specific project, and briefly go through the steps in assessing its social impacts. The first activity is to describe the proposed action. In addition to those listed above, specific examples include the siting of a chemical incinerator, the location of a new manufacturing facility (plant), the development of a state park or other major recreation area. Other examples in rural communities include the siting of a new prison, the opening or closing of a mining facility, the loss of a high school or grade school, or the consolidation of government services. Additional developments include pipelines and gasification plants, the relocation of an existing highway or building new ones, the introduction or expansion of a major business or manufacturing facility. Social impact assessment is also needed when present facilities are expanded, as in the case of building a resort on a reservoir or adding a hazardous landfill to an existing garbage dump. The U.S. Department of Defense does an SIA when a decision is made to close unused military facilities.

📖 *Concepts,* Chapter 6, 15 and 16.

Step 1. Identify Proposed Projects or Policy Changes in Your Community

    A. Name one or more development projects or new policies proposed for your community, region or the areas in which you work.

        1._____

        2._____

    B. In this space write the one for which you will be doing the SIA. _____

_____

Beginning the Scoping Process

Scoping is an early and open process to "scope out" or determine the range of issues to be addressed and for identifying the significant issues related to the proposed action, be it rezoning of property, the building of a destination resort facility or the clean-up of a contaminated site. Scoping also includes identification of the major stakeholders, some preliminary thinking about social impacts and alternatives to the proposed action.

✆ **http://www.epa.gov/compliance/basics/nepa.html** 📖 *Concepts* Chapter 6 ;
For Canada ✆ **www.ec.gc.ca and search on scoping.**

Internal and External Scoping:

● **Internal Scoping** is what you do within your company, agency (ministry) or project team, e.g., project meetings, review of literature, previous completed EIA's or SIA's and your own experience.

_____

_____

● **External Scoping** is obtaining the input of others, e.g., the local community, stakeholders, other agencies, businesses or ministries, outside "experts' or any person or groups that could provide insight into probable future social impacts of the proposed action.

─

_____

_____

Activity 4.2 Purpose and Objective of the <u>Proposed Action</u>

Instructions: In as much detail as possible and based on the preliminary proposal, write a clear statement as to the proposed action. For example, if the decision is to rezone 64 hectares of land from park land to light industrial use, then write that as the decision. If the proposed action is to build a bridge from the mainland to an island, which was previously served by a ferry, write down as many of the details of the decision as possible. If the proposal is to build a prison in your community, then provide as much information about the size and location of the prison as possible.

_____

_____

_____

Activity 4.3 Prepare a Social Profile of the Affected Community

In the previous activity you identified the proposed action for the project or policy that will be the focus of your SIA. Using the four scenarios as a guide, prepare an historical background of the area in as much detail as possible. 📖 *Concepts*, p 69-70; 105-106.

_____

_____

_____

_____

Activity 4.4 Identify the Stage and Time Line for Your Project

Background: In Chapter 3 we talked about stages in project development and that social impacts will be different for different stages and different types of projects (e.g. the building of a road compared with opening a new park). Use the information in Chapter 3 and in the following paragraphs to classify your SIA project by stage and time. Knowing what stages are involved with the proposed policy or project will help in beginning to think about social impacts. Remembering that not all social impacts occur at all stages and you may be asked to assess more than one stage.

Figure 4.1
Stages in Project/Policy Development

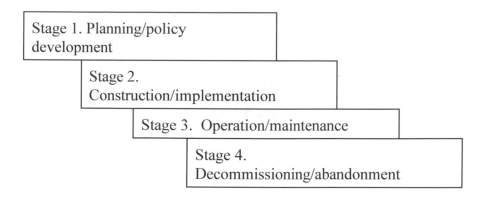

Stage 1. ***Planning/Policy Development*** means all activity that takes place from the time a project or (policy change) is announced to the point where construction or policy implementation begins. Included within this stage are project design, revision, public comment, licensing, the evaluation of alternatives, as well as the decision to go ahead. For example, hearings were conducted in Clark County, Illinois on the application to site a low-level nuclear repository facility outside the Village of Martinsville. Although the permit was eventually denied, social impacts in the form of attitudes toward the project began the day the proposed site was announced. In another example, citizens of Crestview began to think about alternatives for health care services the day hospital closure was first rumored.

Stage 2. ***Construction/implementation*** begins when a decision is made to proceed, a permit is issued, or a law or regulation takes effect. The construction and implementation phase continues through policy implementation or the end of construction. The social impacts taking place during construction will be quite different from those in other phases. In the case of the Eagle Creek Resort on Lake Shelbyville, in East Central Illinois, community leaders in both Shelby and Moultrie counties saw construction jobs as a help to local unemployment. However, because a Union Hall was not present in either county, all the construction workers had to be brought in from St. Louis, Missouri or Terre Haute, Indiana.

Stage 3. ***Operation/maintenance*** is the stage after the construction is complete and /or the policy is fully operational. At this stage **Barn-Wall** is selling merchandise and the **Canadian Dream** development is fully occupied with new residents. Social assessment at this stage should determine if the social and economic impacts (as well as anticipated benefits) that were predicted actually occurred. Most of the long term benefits and consequences of development will occur during the operational phase. In the case of the new prisons in rural areas, most of the social impacts will happen when the facility is fully occupied and family and relatives begin to visit the prisoners.

Stage 4. ***Decommissioning/abandonment*** (***or closure***) begins when the proposal is made that a project/facility will close down or a policy will change at some time in the future. As in the planning stage, the social impacts of decommissioning (e.g., closing Crestview Hospital) begin when the intent to close is announced. The closing of a manufacturing or processing facility can decimate a community, particularly if it has been the single largest employer. At the end of the 20th century, no single event has led to more social impacts in North American rural communities than moving manufacturing facilities off-shore and the consolidation of both agricultural operations and medical facilities.

Step 1.   Place a big ✔ in each box in Figure 4.2 to indicate the stage that applies to your SIA project or policy change.

Figure 4.2
Stages in Project/Policy Development

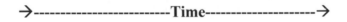

→-------------------------Time--------------------→

Project Name	Planning/Policy Development	Construction/ Implementation	Operation Maintenance	Decommission Abandonment [a]
ACME Waste Mgt. (Siting project)	✔✔	✔✔	✔✔	--
Barn-Wall (New Business)	✔✔	✔✔	✔✔	--
Crestview Hospital (Closing Facility)	—	—	—	✔✔
Canadian Dream (Residential/Recreation)	✔✔	✔✔	✔✔	—
Your Project or Policy _____				

[a] Although not easily shown in schematic stage/time sequence of Figure 4.2, we hope there would be a planning phase before a project is closed down!

Activity 4.5 Establish the Region or Zone of Influence for Your SIA.

At this point in your SIA, you have a clear notion of the <u>proposed action</u>, know more about the history of the area, the stage of your project. Next we need to establish both primary and secondary zones of influence. Let's start by drawing a line around the human communities most affected by the proposed action.

A. **Primary Zone of Influence:** Write a description of the geographical location which you think will be most influenced by the proposed activity. By primary effects, or in the primary zone of influence, we mean direct impacts which will be caused by the <u>proposed action</u> and occur in the same time and location. In the case of a factory closing, workers would be laid off and their families would suffer a loss of income. Unless other work was available nearby, most would have to seek employment elsewhere. ***Remember the observation that biophysical and social impacts are more observable and easily measured at the community and local level.***

Instructions*:* **Primary Zone of Influence** Write down the geographical location for individuals and the community most affected by your project:

_____

_____

_____

_____

_____

B. **Secondary Zone of Influence:** Now write a description of the geographical area which might experience secondary impacts from the proposed action. By secondary effects, we mean the indirect impacts or "effects" which will be caused by the proposed action, but may occur later in time or further removed in distance, but are reasonably foreseeable. For example, the **Canadian Dream** housing development will lead to pressures to rezone adjacent agricultural land to commercial and industrial use to support a larger population.

Instructions: Secondary Zone of Influence List some of the individuals and communities most affected.

_____

_____

_____

Activity 4.6 Identification of Key Stakeholders

Our next step is to locate those individuals, groups, communities, non-governmental organizations, municipal, provincial, and federal governments, private sector organizations and interested citizens most affected by the proposed action. These are called *stakeholders*—or individuals whose daily lives will be altered or in some way have an interest in the proposed action. Some countries use the term *interested and affected parties*. In Chapter 1, we listed major categories of individuals and groups involved in the SIA process: project proponents, the affected community, governmental units at all levels, consultants, and the general public. Use these general categories as a beginning point in identifying stakeholders. The general categories listed below will help you begin to identify and develop information on **key stakeholders**.

Local, Municipal Governments

1._____

2._____

3._____

State, Provincial, Federal Governments

1._____

2._____

3._____

Project Proponents

1._____

2._____

3._____

Community Groups & Organizations

1._____

2._____

3._____

Interested Citizens

1._____

2._____

3._____

Indigenous (Aboriginal) Populations

1._____

2._____

3._____

Special Populations

1._____

2._____

3._____

Step 2. You are almost halfway through the scoping process. You have identified a project for study and the importance of different phases (or stages) in the life of a development project or policy. You have written about the history of the area and a detailed statement of the decision to be made. You have the beginning steps in establishing a boundary around your project area and you have begun to identify the major *stakeholders*—the *interested and affected parties*, those people and communities whose lives will be altered by the proposed action. Before we go further, consider what is meant by social impact assessment and why it is important for both the community and the project proponents! Also think a bit about benefits and consequences for all stakeholders. Write your thoughts in the space below.

_____

_____

_____

_____

_____

_____

_____

_____

_____

On to the next chapter where we will begin the process of identifying social impacts as part of the scoping process.

Chapter 5. Identifying Social Impacts: Scoping Part II

By **social impact assessment (SIA)** we mean identifying and measuring the impacts on the day-to-day quality of life of persons and communities whose environment is affected by a proposed development or policy change.

SIA helps individuals and communities better anticipate the possible social consequences and benefits of a proposed action. You have already established that

....

.... (write your SIA activity here)

may alter the social fabric of life in the community or municipality under study. You have identified the stage in the project, a beginning step in establishing boundaries and identifying some of the key stakeholders. Write in your project/policy change from Chapter 4, Activity 4.1 on the line above.

"Community leaders recognize that social impacts will occur with change. However, it is more difficult for them to identify and explain exactly what those social impacts will be."

You have also learned that doing social impact assessment will alert citizens and community leaders, as well as project proponents, to the likelihood of social changes. Like physical changes in the land, social impacts must be identified and understood. For example, we did not know that certain nitrate compounds from fertilizers contaminated wells in many agricultural areas of the world until research alerted us to the problem. Research on relocation of populations due to water impoundments has show that the older, less educated and minorities have difficulty in adjusting to new locations. Family and friendship ties are lost and are difficult to reestablish if physical barriers are introduced. However, the combination of good planning and knowing about social impacts *in advance* will help communities benefit from such opportunities as a new water and sewage system or cope with the loss of a long time employer.

In this chapter we begin to identify social impacts. For help we turn to decades of research on how policy change and development has altered the social fabric of both urban and rural communities (external scoping). The purpose of the ***Community Guide to Social Impact Assessment*** is just that—a guide to help you know where to look and how to understand social impacts.

➡

Activity 5.1 Case Study: Identify Themes in Your Development Project

Instructions: First let's find out what one group of professional change agents said when asked to talk about social impacts. Five general themes seemed to emerge from our discussion.

1. The first theme included such items as migration to urban areas, crowding, community safety and quality of life (possible population change due to a residential and industrial development).

2. The second theme included such issues as loss of local institutions, lack of individual opportunity, a negative attitude toward change in general, lack of zoning, community development, and specifically, the few job opportunities for youth (possible social changes due to the hospital closing in **Crestview**).

3. The third theme included polarizing of social groups, loss of local control, loss of a traditional life style, and the question...."how will new groups fit into my own community?" (Many of these fears may have been expressed in Island Municipality when the **Canadian Dream** project was announced.)

4. A fourth theme included such factors as a difficult life, personal safety, traffic congestion, as well as such social problems as child abuse, alcoholic and drug abuse, crime and vandalism, teen pregnancy and big welfare rolls. (Our case examples will not deal; with crime and delinquency, but a large influx of outsiders could alter present family and community social relationships.)

5. In a fifth theme, participants mentioned such items as available health care (doctors, dentists and hospitals as well as emergency service and rapid response to trauma incidents), schools to include high educational standards and funding, environmental quality, public transportation facilities, recreation opportunities, senior citizen facilities, clean water and adequate waste disposal facilities. (Certainly, a new residential development and the addition of the **Acme Waste** facility could increase demands on an antiquated community infrastructure.)

Step 1. Discuss the five themes with someone from your study area and decide which theme (as well as others) describes your project (external scoping). Record a summary of your discussion here to include new themes.

_____

_____

_____

_____

_____

Activity 5.2 Try Your Hand at Possible Social Impacts

Now let's focus on the proposed change in your community. What do you see as the likely social impacts or the "effects" of the proposed action? Write in the spaces below–along with a sentence or two of elaboration. This part of scoping asks you to begin identifying possible impacts (based on internal scoping). Remember to focus on social impacts rather than biological or physical land use changes.

SOCIAL IMPACTS	BRIEF DESCRIPTION
1._____	_____
_____	_____
2._____	_____
_____	_____
3. _____	_____
_____	_____
4. _____	_____
_____	_____
5._____	_____
_____	_____

Activity 5.3 Learning About the Key Social Impact Assessment Variables

I have placed my 28 social impact assessment variables under the five categories shown in Figure 5.1. Community development practitioners and planners as well as community leaders have a general understanding of the categories and relate to the labels for the individual SIA variables.

Figure 5.1
Categories Important to Social Impact Assessment (SIA)

1. Population Impacts
2. Community/Institutional Arrangements
3. Communities in Transition
4. Individual and Family Level Impacts
5. Community Infrastructure Needs

---

1. **Population Impacts** means changes in the number, density and distribution of people (e.g., rural to urban), the rate of influx or out migration and any changes in the composition of the population in terms of residence, age, ethnicity and gender.

   Population impact variables are:
   - Population impacts, SIA#1.
   - Influx and/or out flux of temporary workers, SIA#2.
   - Presence of seasonal (leisure) residents, SIA#3.
   - Relocation of individuals and families, SIA#4.
   - Dissimilarity in age, gender, racial or ethnic composition, SIA#5.

2. **Community/Institutional Arrangements** means changes in attitudes and values, the emergence of interest groups as well as changes in local government and employment opportunities for all citizens.

   Included in Community/Institutional Arrangements are the following specific variables:

   - Formation of attitudes toward the project, SIA#6.
   - Interest group activity, SIA#7.
   - Alteration in size and structure of local government, SIA#8.
   - Presence of planning and zoning activities, SIA#9.
   - Industrial diversification, SIA#10.
   - Living/ Family Wage, SIA#11.
   - Enhanced economic inequities, SIA#12.
   - Change in employment equity of minority groups, SIA#13.
   - Changing occupational opportunities, SIA#14.

3.   **Communities in Transition** refer to changes in community image, the alteration in community power structure with the arrival or departure of businesses or governmental agencies and any conflict that might arise between local residents and newcomers or even outsiders as the result of a development project or policy change.

Included in this category are the following specific variables:
- Presence of an outside agency, SIA#15.
- Inter-organizational cooperation, SIA#16.
- Introduction of new social classes, SIA#17.
- Change in the commercial/industrial focus of the community, SIA#18.
- Presence of weekend residents (recreational), SIA#19.

4.   **Individual and Family Level Impacts** means changes in family structure, individual social relations and how the proposed action is perceived to change the daily lives of individuals and families in the area.

Included in individual and family level impacts are the following variables:
- Disruption in daily living and movement patterns, SIA#20.
- Dissimilarity in religious practices, SIA#21.
- Alteration in family structure, SIA#22.
- Disruption in social networks, SIA#23.
- Perceptions of public health and safety, SIA#24.
- Change in leisure opportunities, SIA#25.

5.   **Community Infrastructure Needs** means changes in everything from kilometers of roads to greater sewage capacity to the need for more police units that might be altered as the result of the proposed action. This cluster of variables also includes changes in land use.

Included in community infrastructure needs are the following variables:

- Change in community infrastructure, SIA#26.
- Land acquisition and disposal, SIA#27.
- Effects of known cultural, historical, sacred and archaeological resources, SIA#28.

Activity 5.4 A First Cut: Which of the 28 variables might apply?

After reading through the list of 28 Social Impact Assessment variables, ask which ones might apply to your project setting?

Step 1. It might help to take notes about how these variables relate to your project.

_____

_____

_____

_____

_____

Without turning to Chapters 7 through 11, write down at least five from the list of 28 SIA variables which you think might be involved in the way of a social impact. Before beginning, think about what is meant by a social impact or an effect? "Affecting" means "will or may have an effect on". Remember that *direct (primary) effects*, are caused by the proposed action and appear in the same time and place. *Secondary (indirect) effects*, are also caused by the action but appear later in time, or are further removed in distance, but are reasonably foreseeable. In the **Gateway Pacific Terminal** SIA, described in Chapter 15 of 📖 *Concepts,* an indirect effect would be other heavy industry which might locate in the area to service the commercial needs of the terminal and port facilities.

Ranking of Social Impact Variables for Your Project

<u>Rank</u>	<u>SIA#</u>	<u>Variable Name</u>
1.		
2.		
3.		
4.		
5.		

Activity 5.5 Review What You Have Learned About the Importance of Using Social Impact Assessment in the Planning Process by Explaining the Benefits of a Social Impact Assessment to another person .Include possible components of a social profile.

Step 1.   Write your observations in the space below about how the community might benefit from conducting an SIA for the project you have identified.

_____

_____

_____

_____

_____

_____

_____

Step 2.   This exercise on internal scoping represents the beginning of your community social profile. Write down some of the SIA variables to be including in the baseline study.

_____

_____

_____

_____

_____

_____

_____

Activity 5.6 Think about alternatives. In the spirit of the planning process consider different ways to accomplish the <u>proposed action</u> with fewer resources and fewer impacts on the human and biophysical environment.

So take a moment and think about alternatives. How could we achieve the same goals and objectives of the <u>proposed action</u>? Write your ideas the space below as we will need them when we attempt mitigation and alternatives in Chapter 13.

_____

_____

_____

_____

_____

Review of Chapters 4 and 5

1. **T or F**   The key to doing a good SIA is to understand the <u>proposed action</u>.

2. **T or F**   Understanding the project stage makes it much easier to identify possible social impacts.

3. **T or F**   Secondary social impacts occur later in time or are further removed in distance but are reasonably foreseeable.

4. **T or F**   Stakeholders are individuals, groups and organizations whose daily lives will be most affected by the proposed project.

5. **T or F**   Population impacts refer in part to changes in numbers, density and the distribution of the population.

6. **T or F**   Not all social impacts occur all the time or in each SIA setting.

7.   Name the two types of scoping: .... and ....

On to Chapter 6 where we begin to learn about the sources of information to measure social impact assessment variables and review some notes about methods and measurement.

➡

Chapter 6. Locating the Information to Measure Social Impacts: Scoping Part III

The objectives of this chapter are:

1. To establish some boundaries around your SIA project; (We began the process in Chapter 4 when we talked about primary and secondary zones of influence.)

2. To help you begin to locate the information that you will need to work through Chapters 7 through 11;

3. To outline some approaches to determining significant social impacts;

4. To write down important basic information about your community— all of which will be used in later portions of this workbook;

5. To talk about some of the myths that surrounds the use of social impact assessment in the planning process.

Fortunately, much of the data, to include basic population profiles and needs assessment information, will be available from sources at the local level. *It is important to remember that rural sociologists, agricultural economists, planners, and community development professionals often use the same data, but analyze and interpret the information in very different ways!* Therefore, by working with these different approaches, both the SIA practitioner and the community will have a better and more comprehensive picture of what is happening as a result of the proposed action.

Chapter 6 is the last part of the formal ***SCOPING PROCESS***—locating the information to analyze the SIA variables. Chapter 13, in this workbook, outlines the basics of a social impact management plan (SIMP)—However, *The Community Guide to Social Impact Assessment* really is the work plan; and includes all the guidelines necessary to manage social impacts.

➡

Activity 6.1 Establish the Boundaries of Your Social Impact Assessment

Understanding Levels of Local Government

♦The **Township** (36 sq. miles) is the smallest unit in terms of the activities of any level of government in U.S. counties. As a result, little information is collected or available at this level. Townships may be responsible for collecting property taxes, maintaining township roads and assisting welfare recipients. Some have volunteer fire departments.

♦The **Village** is the smallest level of municipal government in most states and provinces. Social impacts are easy to identify at the village level, but data are not always available and ffeasily accessible.

♦A **City** or **municipality** is an incorporated area of at least 2,500 persons (in some parts of the U.S. they are called boroughs, towns or parishes). The larger the city, the more data are available. If the municipality is large enough, e.g., at least 10,000 persons, data will be reported for both census tracts and census city blocks. In Canada, many local governmental units have been combined into municipalities for efficiency in administration. In other countries, shires or parishes are the basic administrative units.

♦The **County** is the smallest unit of government in most U.S. states where all state, federal and census data are reported. In countries using the British Towne Planning System, shires are equivalent to counties.

Understanding other types of jurisdictional units

A. **Tribal land** refers to indigenous, tribal or First Nations which have separate nation status. These jurisdictions are common in the U.S. and Canada and increasingly in countries where indigenous populations are seeking control over their traditional lands. http://www.census.gov/geo/maps-data/data/tiger-cart-boundary.html

B. **Authorities and National Boards** have special jurisdictional powers that overlap governmental units. For example, Port Authorities operate water and air transport facilities. Authorities also exist for development and maintenance of energy and recreational facilities, inland waterways and housing.

C. **State, Provincial and Federal Land Management Agencies** refer to governmental units which operate and manage public lands. Examples include federal and state forest lands, national parks, and military installations.

D. **Special Districts** include for example, water districts, flood control districts, cemetery districts and when they cross municipal boundaries, school and park districts.

Step 1. Obtain a Large Scale County or Municipality Map

A. On a detailed map of your county, municipality or shire, showing township, municipal, village or borough boundaries, draw a line around the area where you think the primary impacts (influences, issues, effects, etc.,) of your SIA might extend. Let's call the enclosed area *project boundaries*. Oftentimes retail trade and public transport areas provide a good delineation for primary zones of influence.

B. Trace the boundaries for the townships, villages, cities, municipalities, boroughs, shires, towns and counties (if more than one) that lie within the project boundaries.

C. If present, trace the boundaries of tribal lands, authorities, as well as other state, provincial and federal jurisdictions.

Step 2. Understand Sources of Information Available to You

All of the social impact assessment variables listed in Chapter 5 require data that may be available at the county and municipality level. Most census data, as well as vital statistics, deeds, building and zoning codes, among others, as used by local, state, provincial and federal agencies, are available at the county and municipal level and may include data for small villages and towns. Census tract and block data are available for both rural and urban areas. Public meetings, newspaper articles, and transcripts of meetings are a source of ethnographic data. The measurement of SIA variables also requires information about proposed project design which should be obtained early in the planning stage from the project proponent or sponsor. Sources of information include but are not limited to:

📄 **Project Parameter** information may be obtained directly from the proponent or gathered from on-site visits. Example types of data include numbers of construction workers, length of construction, size and boundaries of project as well as the projected number and type of permanent and part-time employees. **Cooperation of the project proponent is crucial to a successful SIA. Obtain the support of the proponent early in the assessment process.**

👫 **Census and Other Demographic Statistics** information is available from the federal and provincial census of Population Characteristics, Housing, Agriculture and Business, Bureau of Business Affairs, Vital Statistics, Bureau of Labor Statistics, and other public and quasi-public organizations that routinely collect statistical data about the general population. In the U.S. go to **www.census.gov/**, in Canada go to **www.statscan.gc.ca/**. The United Nations provides links to census data for all member countries. **http://unstats.un.org/unsd/methods/inter-natlinks/sd_natstat.asp** Most include the information in several languages including English. 📖 *Concepts,* Chapters 2, 3, 7and 9. In the space below write the name of the nearest regional library that archives public documents and census information.

County/Municipal/Village/Township/Shire data include details on government activity available from local and regional planning offices, school records, tax records, zoning and land use information, unemployment data, land ownership records, utilities and numbers and types of local government employees, as well as information on everything from building permits to welfare expenditures. For examples of data available at the municipal and county level go to **http://www.co.whatcom.wa.us/index.jsp** or **www.cob.org**

Secondary Materials is a catch-all category to include everything from the commercial pages of telephone books to environmental and social impact statements that have been written about similar projects. Many land management, energy and regulatory agencies keep extensive records on such diverse activities as recreational visits, building permits, energy production, grazing permits, crime statistics, health statistics, and disease and incident exposure. Search the on-line directories of the municipalities and counties in your area for these types of data.

Community Observations means keeping your eyes open and talking with people in coffee shops, pubs and other public gathering places as well as by watching live television coverage of community activities, attending community meetings and other local gatherings. Observational data increases the understanding of possible effects of the proposed action on your community. Windshield surveys provide good first impressions. Look for boarded up shops. Is the area prosperous or run down? Note the ethnic, racial and age composition of people on the streets.

Public Participation Information Your project may have or will be the topic of public hearings or meetings. In the formalized EIA process, this is called *external scoping*. In such cases, valuable information about community attitudes and perceptions about the proposed action may be obtained both by attending and conducting public meetings and reading the transcripts. Other sources of data include interviews with key informants, newspaper accounts and letters in local newspapers and if available, public opinion surveys. Most local and regional libraries and planning departments collect and organize articles about important present and upcoming development activity. *Concepts*, Chapters 17, 18 and 19 and **www.iap2.org**

Local Knowledge refers to information and understanding about the state of the biophysical and social environments that have been acquired by the people of a community which hosts (or will host) the proposed action. It may be unique features that would make a project difficult to get under way or even complete. Local knowledge can only be obtained by consultation with the local population during the initial design phase and while preparing the terms of reference for the environmental and social impact assessment.

Although obtaining data and information about your community is time consuming and may be frustrating, remember, however, that in the process you will get to know the community and region much better.

Activity 6.2 Obtaining Baseline Data at County/Municipal and Shire Offices

Instructions: As you begin your social assessment, locate the various local governmental offices that will provide much of your data. Developing the social profile and the baseline study will help you begin to think about the area and the information you need to gather.

Step 1 First go to the Municipal or County Planning Department and find information on the six (6) top issues or needs that have been identified for your study area (e.g., needed job opportunities, aging population, and urban sprawl).

1._____   4._____

2._____   5._____

3. _____   6._____

Step 2 Next, go to the census website or the city/county data book to find the population for 1990, 2000, 2010, 2015 and estimates for 2025 and 2030 (or beyond).

_____	_____	_____	_____	_____	_____
1990	2000	2010	2015	2025	2030

Step 3 Again, from the recent census, the city/county data book, planning department or public library, determine the location of information on income levels, sector employment and local tax base. Write the location of the tax assessor and website for your community below, e.g., **http://www.co.whatcom.wa.us/index.jsp**

_____

Step 4 From the county/municipality/shire tax collection office you can obtain information on the numbers of different types of firms and establishments as well as the types of jobs and employment categories. Enter the number of retail firms and establishments in your community_____.

Step 5 Next, from the Office of Employment/Economic Security (unemployment office) obtain details on the make-up of the unemployed labor force in your area. Write the number of unemployed persons in your study area in this space

_____.

Step 6 Each countries have labeled political jurisdictions according to trade, manufacturing and agriculture activities. Write in the space below how you would label your community (e.g., agriculture, mixed industrial, etc.)?

_____

Overview of Your Study Area

The People	The Numbers
Median age: _____	Incorporated (year):_____
Public school enrollment (K-12):_____	Miles² or Kilometers ²: _____
% Completed College:_____	Population: _____
% Families below poverty level:_____	Median family income:_____
% Home ownership:_____	Median house value:_____
% Renters: _____	Rental housing units:_____
% Minorities: _____	Parks (acres or hectares):_____

Ethnic (Racial) Makeup

Ethnic(Racial) Makeup

Indigenous 2%

White 25.4%

Asian/Pacific Islander 54%

Other .6%

Black 18%

Map of your Study Area

The information you obtain in answering the above questions is an example of the type of data you will be gathering and analyzing in Chapters 7-11. One of the goals of *The Community Guide to Social Impact Assessment* is <u>to help you use information close at hand to better understand changes taking place in the impacted community</u>. The Social Profile and Baseline Study provide a nice composite picture of your community.

Activity 6.3 Methods for Determining the Significance of Social Impacts. Projection of Estimated Effects

In the next five chapters, probable social impacts will be formulated in terms of predicted conditions without the proposed action (baseline) and social impacts which can be interpreted as the differences between the future, with and without the proposed action (**The Comparative Approach**). The analytical procedure is based on the **comparative social impact assessment model** outlined in Chapter 3. Methods of projecting the future lie at the heart of your social impact assessment, and much of the process of analysis is tied up in this endeavor. The methods used for projecting and determining significance fall into the following categories:

- *Thresholds of Change* refers to quantitative measures of change in a resident population, associated with a proposed action (increase or decrease). Adjustment to population change above or below a threshold (generally 5% or 10% depending upon the size of the community) will influence a community's capacity to absorb newcomers or deal with the loss of social capital with persons leaving the area. A community's physical infrastructure as well as the viability of community services may also be affected by population change.

- *Straight-line trend projections* means taking an existing trend and simply projecting at the same rate of change into the future. We assume that what happened in the past is likely to happen in the future. For example, recreation visitations increase each year at about the same rate they did in the past.

- *Population multiplier methods* means designated multiples for such SIA variables, as job opportunities, housing units and infrastructure needs resulting from an increase or decrease in identified or projected population change.

- *Statistical significance* means calculations to determine probabilistic differences between the impacted area with and without the proposed action. A social assessor may employ comparative statistical methods to determine statistical significance for certain SIA variables.

- *Scenarios* are *logical-imaginations* based on construction of hypothetical futures through a process of *mentally modeling* the assumptions about the SIA variables in question.

- *Expert judgment* Persons familiar with the study area could be asked to present scenarios and assess the significant consequences of the proposed action.

- *Calculation of "futures foregone"* A number of methods have been formulated to determine what options would be given up irrevocably as a result of a plan or project. Examples would be the loss of river recreation and agricultural land after the building of water impoundments. The wetlands mitigation strategy outlined in Chapter 13 is an example of an attempt to reduce/mitigate "futures foregone."

- *A Red Flag of Significant Social Impacts* would be the destruction of sacred sites of Indigenous people or restricting and disturbing their traditional fishing and hunting grounds. A proposed action would be found to be significant impact if

As you complete a social impact assessment, remember that the smaller the government unit for which social impact assessment information is obtained, the more readily the data are observed, understood and measured.

critical areas are disturbed such as habitat for endangered species or wetlands critical for maintaining water quality.

• ***Community Members Think it is Significant*** If during the scoping process, local stakeholders identify and suggest a social impact, then it becomes significant and must be addressed and measured. "If perceived to be real, than the event or situation is real in all its consequences (W.I. Thomas).

Activity 6.4 Dealing with the Controversy Surrounding Social Impact Assessment

Before we move to the detailed analysis of the social impact assessment variables, we need to understand the key reasons for doing SIA. The effective social assessor must understand the benefits and be familiar with arguments both for and against SIA. Now that you have an idea of how to proceed in doing an SIA, you will be asked by others in your community why is SIA important and how will conducting a social impact assessment help the community in planning for future change? The following are "myths" or reasons for *not* doing a social impact assessment. Each ***myth*** is followed by explanations about the importance of doing an SIA in your community. These reasons may be helpful in explaining the process to other professionals, practitioners as well as leaders in your community!

Figure 6.2 Five Myths about SIA

1. **Social impacts are common sense and everybody should know what they are.**
2. **Social impacts cannot be measured and, therefore, should be ignored.**
3. **Social impacts seldom occur--therefore, it is a waste of time to consider them.**
4. **Social impacts deal with "costs," not "benefits" and therefore, the assessment slows or stops "development".**
5. **Social impact assessment simply increases the price of the project and will not improve benefits.**

Responding to Myths about Social Impact Assessment

1. **Social impacts are common sense and everyone knows what they are.** *Knowledge is the forerunner of common sense.* The benefits and consequences of water impoundments are now quite predictable—but only after four decades of follow-up studies. The SIA process also includes using local knowledge in the decision process. The social learning that takes place is a two way street. Project planners can provide the research background to assist in community understanding. However, the local community can take that information, modify it and add to it based on knowledge of the local situation. One of the purposes of social impact assessment is to look at past projects in your community and those in similar communities and turn knowledge of social impacts into common sense so that they might be understood by all citizens in your community.

2. **Social impacts cannot be measured and, therefore, should be ignored.** *I contend that one can always find an indicator!* It may be qualitative, as a change in public concern over health risks from polluted groundwater or radioactive releases. It may be quantitative, as the number of teachers required to raise literacy levels or population increases resulting from a destination tourist facility—but each will have an indicator. As you will find in working through this book, many social impacts are easily understood and ways of measuring them can be demonstrated in a variety of settings, because the information is close at hand.

3. **Social impacts seldom occur--therefore, it is a waste of time to consider them.** *Social impacts like biophysical and financial impacts __always occur__, but __may not__ always be significant!* Road building in rural communities disrupts daily living and movement patterns, but the long run benefits include access to outside employment, markets and reduced isolation. The loss of 300 jobs in a community of 3,000 people is a very significant social impact. On the other hand, the opening of a *bed and breakfast facility*, while providing some employment for one family, may not significantly alter the social fabric of the community.

4. **Social impacts deal with "costs," not "benefits" and therefore, the assessment slows or stops development projects.** Change of any kind brings *social costs to some and social benefits to others*, no matter what the size of the community or the nature of the proposed action. This analogy is similar to the ideas behind cost-benefit analysis used in economics. The costs of building the project are weighed against the benefits, and if the benefits come out on top, the decision is generally made to go ahead. Building an access road to a garbage dump around the town was more expensive, but improved company/community relations and reduced in-town traffic congestion. In another road project, systematic involvement of the local communities allowed engineers to design a route that was both cheaper and supported by the affected communities. As a by-product, the previously skeptical highway engineers became convinced of the importance of citizen involvement in the planning process. However, you should remember that the *social costs* are almost always borne at the community or local level. *Economic benefits* tend to be sold on a multi-county or at the provincial level.

"The purpose of (*social*)impact assessment is to turn insight into foresight" Helge Lund, President of Statoil, 23 May, 2006 in the keynote address before the International Association for Impact Assessment (IAIA), Stavanger Forum, Stavanger, Norway.

The US Congress passed the 1969 NEPA legislation, in large degree, because environmental and social costs to local communities were not included in the planning/decision process. In the planning process, it is important to know which groups and individuals will benefit from the proposed development or policy change. When a pulp mill, a heavy polluter is closed, the social costs may be devastating to local community residents. At the same time downstream, residents may have cleaner water and new technology may mean a cheaper paper product.

5. **Social impact assessment simply increases the price of the project and will not improve benefits.** *If an SIA is conducted as an integral part of an EIA or other decision making process, and when it is oriented towards problem solving it is a powerful tool.* I maintain that in the long run, social impact assessment

saves money, improves the likelihood that the <u>proposed action</u> will be successful and that the community will adjust better to any economic and political loss. A major benefit of the SIA process is allowing the affected populations to understand, participate in and cope with a proposed action. The SIA process allows the social concerns of the entire community to be considered at every stage of the planning process—not *after* the decision. *The principal of free prior and informed consent.* The purpose of this book is to alert local leaders to the variety of impacts and changes that might occur as a result of project development and/or policy change. Such information will insure that promised benefits are realized and any negative consequences are understood and addressed in advance.

Before you begin the detailed analysis of the 28 Social Impact Assessment variables, test your knowledge of common acronyms in the field of social and environmental impact assessment.

EIS_____

ESIA_____

SIA_____

ADB_____

IBA_____

SEA_____

SEIA_____

HIA_____

IIA_____

TOR_____

FONSI_____

IAIA_____

On to Measuring and Understanding Social Impacts

Chapter 7. Population Impacts

How will the proposed action impact the human population in your community?

The objective of this chapter is to help you obtain information on five social impact assessment variables to determine if **population impacts** will occur as a result of the action you have selected to assess. By **population impacts** we mean changes in the number, density and distribution of people, the rate of influx or out-migration (e.g. rural to urban) as well as any changes in the composition of the population, to include age, gender, race and ethnic origin.

At the end of Chapter 6, you obtained some baseline population data for your study area. That information will be put to use in Chapter 7.

➡

SIA 1. Assessing Population Change

Instructions: **Why is population change important?** The magnitude and rate of population change is a driving force behind community infrastructure and service requirements and may be a major determinant of other financial and social impacts in the project area. Three key indicators of population change are used in this *Guide*:

(1) the size of population change;
(2) the density of population in the assessment area; and
(3) the rate of influx or outflux of persons due to,
    for example, construction or other project related activity.

Step 1. **Using Historical Information from the Available Census.** Enter the population history of your community from Chapter 6.

_____	_____	_____	_____	_____	_____	_____
1990	2000	2010	2015	2025	2030	

In the U.S. go to **www.census.gov/**. (Enter TIGER for U.S. data by geographical area.)
In Canada go to **www.statscan.gc.ca/**. The United Nations provides links to census data for all member countries:
⚙ **http://unstats.un.org/unsd/methods/inter-natlinks/sd_natstat.asp**
The American community survey updates population information between census periods
⚙ **http://www.census.gov/acs/www/** Some Regional libraries carry census publications:
📖 U.S. Bureau of the Census. *Statistical Abstract* and *County and City Data Book*.

Step 2. **Questions to guide the analysis of population impacts.**

A. Has the project area experienced population decline, stayed about the same or increased over the past 30-40 years?

Declined ___ Stayed the Same ___ Increased ___

B. Based on discussion with area leaders or information obtained from planning documents; What are the population goals for the area?

Continue to grow ___ Remain the same ___ Stop the decline ___

Step 3. **Tabulate population changes in your study area.**

A. Complete Table 7.1 on population change for your assessment area using the **Crestview Hospital** example as a guide.

B. For example, the 2000 population of Crestview was 9,400, with the hospital employing a total of 340 persons all living in the community. When the hospital closes, 340 people will be unemployed. We estimate that 80% of the employees representing 272 households will leave the community to find employment. As a result we estimate that 680 persons will move from Crestview leading to a 7% decline in population.

Certain assumptions were involved in our estimates. The nearest moderate-sized hospital is located 45 miles away, with a major medical facility 72 miles away in the opposite direction. Not all 340 employees will be hired by the moderate-sized hospital, nor will many of the employees be willing or able to commute 90 minutes to the larger facility. There are few alternative employment opportunities in Crestview as a large manufacturing plant closed two years ago. As a result most former hospital employees must leave the community.

Therefore we estimate that 80% of the 340 employees will leave Crestview in search of new employment. We also assumed that each employee represents the average household size of 2.5 persons based on the recent census (our first use of multipliers). Therefore 2.5 times 340 indicate a loss of 680 persons or a 7% decline in the resident population. Population density in Crestview decreases from 9400/3 to 8720/3 persons per square mile. The incorporated area of Crestview is about 3 square miles.

Table 7.1 Population Change

	Your Community	Crestview Hospital
Present Population	_____	9400
Estimated Population Following Project	_____	8720
Difference (+ or -)	_____	-680
% Change	_____	-7%

Step 4. **Enter significant results**

If the increase or decrease is greater than 5%, research has shown that the area may experience significant population impacts. If the total community/municipal area is larger than 10,000 persons use the 500 number to determine significance. Enter both the number and the percent change in population on page 136, Chapter 12. Population numbers may be needed for other SIA variables.

Interpret the results of your analysis for SIA #1_____

_____

_____

SIA 2. Assessing the Influx or Outflux of Temporary Workers

Instructions: **Why are temporary increases or decreases in population important?**

Many social impacts can be traced to the number and occupational composition of construction and associated workers that would be required to build (or dismantle) a proposed or built facility. Social impacts due to the influx of workers may be temporary (i.e., housing and health care), while other changes (such as infrastructure expansion) may be permanent. For example, at Lake Shelbyville in Central Illinois, the temporary construction workers required not only more housing, but more police and additional health facilities (all requiring increased local expenditures).

The proposed development of a major retail outlet, **Barn-Wall**, provides an example of social impacts that might occur during the *Construction/Implementation* phase. The project would require a work force of approximately 55 persons for 9-12 months.

To estimate the number of construction workers to be hired from within the community, the assessor needs to know if a local contractor will do the project. If not, find out if it is a Union contract and if a Union Hall is located in the project community. If not, it is unlikely that a significant portion of the construction workers would be hired from the community. In the Lake Shelbyville example cited above, there were no Union workers available in the two-county area, so all the workers had to be brought in from the outside—thus an important financial benefit of jobs for the community workers was lost. In growth areas, such as the construction of LNG pipelines and refineries in remote areas of Western and Northern Canada, new projects compete for scarce labor, driving up project costs.

In the **Barn-Wall** example, the village population is 3,700, and no local contractor is large enough to handle a project of this size. Therefore, most construction workers would be hired from outside the community.

Step 1. **Obtaining information on temporary workers**

Data on the number and occupational composition of construction and associated workers may be obtained from the project proponent. Two types of occupational profiles will be necessary to complete a later section of this guide—construction workers and permanent employees. Here we use temporary construction workers.

Does the proposed project require increased numbers of workers during a construction phase? Yes ☐   No ☐.

If No, go to SIA #3, If Yes, obtain the necessary information to answer the questions in Table 7.2 on the next page.

Table 7.2
Construction Worker Trends

	Your Community	Barn-Wall Store
Average # Workers/Month	_____	55
Average # Workers Hired from Outside/Month	_____	50
% Workers Hired from Outside the Community/Month	_____	90%
Length of Construction Period	_____	11 months

Step 2.   **Enter significant results**

If the number of workers recruited from outside the primary and secondary zones of influence is greater than 40 or 25 percent and/or the construction period is greater than six months, please enter this information on page 136, in Chapter 12.

Help: Algorithms that assist in developing a "construction worker profile" are available to predict their financial contribution and estimated infrastructure needs in the area. Input requires the numbers and types of workers, the cost of the construction and the availability of materials locally and the estimated length of the project (☐Leistritz and Murdock, 1981). Output includes the expenditures and tax revenues that will remain in the area. However, these calculations, as well as others throughout this workbook, require the cooperation of the project proponents. Such cooperation is not always forthcoming.

Notes: **In the space below explain how you obtained data for SIA #2. Also detail any difficulties you experienced in getting information from the project proponent.**

_____

_____

_____

_____

SIA 3. Assessing the Presence of Seasonal (Leisure) Residents

Definition: The presence of seasonal (leisure) residents refers to a permanent but seasonal increase or decrease in population resulting from, for example, opening a new recreational opportunity or seasonal home development.

Instructions: **Why is information on seasonal or temporary residents important?**

Recreational and tourism related infrastructure development means more on and off site recreational or seasonal housing needs. These needs may lead to the building of mobile homes, motels, gas stations and other commercial activities on nearby land. Such activity may enhance or detract from the anticipated benefits if local planning is inadequate or has not been implemented. If the numbers of seasonal residents are high, the identity and occupational opportunities in the community may increasingly be restricted to and rely upon the presence of seasonal residents and visitors. Occupational opportunities may be limited to seasonal employment rather than full paying year round employment.

> "Destination Resort Facilities may lead to big social class differences between very high income non-resident owners and working class seasonally employed residents."

The fluctuation in the population of a community is likely to have a substantial effect on the community's infrastructure, employment patterns, business practices and other aspects of daily living. Examples include high cyclical unemployment, service shortages, negative aesthetic impacts and severe traffic congestion. Other examples of seasonal residents include migrant agricultural workers, seasonal forest and fisheries workers, as well as retirees and even college students. Seasonal residents generally require the same services as permanent residents, but not year round. Thus employment is seasonal and facilities are underused.

In the **Canadian Dream** example, we estimate the total population at final build out to be about 6,000. Based on similar projects on mainland Vancouver, it is estimated that 100% of the condominiums, 75% of the townhouses, as well as 25% of the single family residences will be marketed to seasonal residents. We estimate seasonal residents at 3,325, which is 54% of the projected population of the entire development and about 70% of the current population of Island Municipality.

Step 1. **Obtaining data on seasonal residents**

A. Based on your understanding of the proposed project in your area, will it bring seasonal (leisure) residents to the community? Yes ☐ No☐; If No, go to SIA #4.

B. If seasonal residents are expected, estimate the number from information obtained about the project proponent and enter in Table 7.3 on the next page (estimated). Sources of data on seasonal residents include developer proposals, utility accounts, resort records, college enrollments, agricultural employment records, visitor estimates, addresses for property tax billing, and other types of enrollment data obtained at the county, shire, municipal or provincial level.

Table 7.3
Seasonal Residents

	Your Community	Canadian Dream Development
Current Population	_____	4,700
Seasonal Residents 54% of total population of Canadian Dream at build out of 6,088)	_____	3,325
% of Seasonal Residents to Current Population	_____	70%

Sources of information for recreational and seasonal residents

- www.discoveramerica.com Only limited estimates of visitors to national parks, destination resorts and recreation areas, to include cruise ship and airline passenger numbers are avaiable. Unfortunately, data may only come from commercial sources and local visitor bureaus.
- Statistics Canada at www.statscan.ca (visitors to recreation areas)

Step 2.   **Enter significant results.**

If the proposed project will bring seasonal residents and or visitors to the area, your community will experience significant variations in employment oppotunities! If expected seasonal or temporary residents as a percent of the permanent population is greater than 10 percent and/or 400 persons, enter this information in Chapter 12 on page 137.

Interpret the results of your analysis for SIA #3

_____

_____

_____

_____

SIA 4. Identifying Individuals and Families to be Relocated

Definition: This SIA variable refers to the number of persons who will be permanently relocated from their present homes, either voluntarily or involuntarily, as a result of the proposed action.

Instructions: **Why is the relocation of families and individuals important?**

> "The purpose of this chapter is to determine if population impacts will occur-not measure and analyze in depth the actual impacts."

Whether voluntary or involuntary, any type of relocation is stressful for the individuals and families involved. For planning purposes, the severity of the impact generally depends both on the numbers of persons to be relocated as well as the distance they must move. A compounding factor is the time lapse from first announcement until the move actually takes place. In the case of Lake Shelbyville in Central Illinois, U.S.A., we found that the elderly, poor, and long-time residents along the Kaskaskia River suffered the most from displacement, because re-establishing former life and friendship support systems was difficult. In addition, poorer families lacked the resources to deal with the social cost of moving.

📖 *Concepts,* Chapter 14.

In one of our study examples, **Acme Waste Management** has taken an option on 1,200 acres (of which 450 will be used for the landfill), just north of Arvana. Within the option area are six farmhouses, as well as 20 families in a small mobile home park. Using our standard multiplier of 2.5 persons per household, we estimate that approximately 65 persons will be relocated to make room for the waste facility.

Step 1.   **Procedures for analyzing the relocation variable**.

A. Do you anticipate that individuals and families will be relocated as a result of the proposed project? Yes ☐   No ☐.
If No, go on to SIA #5.

B. If yes, from a map of the area or information obtained from the project proponent, estimate the number of households that will be *relocated* as a result of the proposed project and complete the table below using the **Acme Waste Management** example. (These data may be obtained from the project proponent or map overlays showing residential and commercial building locations.)

C. From census information and data about the households, how many of the persons to be relocated would be considered elderly, poor and/or long term residents of the area? Enter that estimate _____(#) and the percent of that number of the total relocated _____(%).

D. Is the move voluntary ☐ ?   or involuntary ☐ ?
The Asian Development Bank has excellent guidelines on involuntary relocation: ☝ **www.adb.org/documents/handbook-resettlement-guide-good-practice**

For other sources of data on involuntary relocation go to ⚓**http://www.shelterlibrary.org** or goggle "Forced Relocation" and/or "Eminent Domain."

E. Are plans included in the project to provide housing for these persons in the immediate vicinity of their present home?

Yes ☐   No ☐.

Table 7.4
Relocation of Families and Individuals

	Your Community	**Acme Waste Site**
Households relocated	_____	26
Persons relocated	_____	65
Number elderly, poor, long-term residents	_____	26
Elderly & poor as a percent of persons relocated	_____	40%
Time from first hearing until final move	_____	22 months

Step 2. **Enter significant results**

If more than 25 persons (ten households) are to be relocated and more than 40 percent of these persons are elderly, poor or long-term residents, and housing is not available in the immediate area, expect the displaced persons to have adjustment problems. Research has shown that stress from uncertainty becomes a serious problem if the move does not occur within 18 months of announcement. Enter the results from table 7.4 in Chapter 12, on page 137.

Interpret the results of your analysis for SIA #4

_____

_____

SIA 5. *Assessing the Dissimilarity in Age, Gender, Racial and Ethnic Composition*

Definition: SIA #5 refers to the introduction into the project area of a sizable category of persons dissimilar to the resident population in one or more of the characteristics of age, gender, race or ethnicity.

Instruction: **What social impacts might occur if newcomers differ in age, race or ethnic origin from local residents?** One of the goals of community development is to enhance benefits with minimal social disruption. Bringing in persons, whose backgrounds differ from the population of the community, may necessitate changes in community infrastructure and the provision of support services to meet the needs of diverse populations. Other social impacts may include disruption of social relationships and traditional power structures and problems of newcomer integration into the community. During construction of the Central Highlands water diversion project in Lesotho (Southern Africa) many unemployed Black males from the surrounding states and countries flocked to the area. They built and lived in squatter housing which upset the family structure of many local villages. Crime and prostitution increased dramatically and the HIV virus became widespread.

The **Canadian Dream** residential development will require a large number of construction workers from outside the community and should take at least 10 years to complete. Most of these workers will be under 35 and many will be Black and others of Asian origin. While some will be married, they will not bring their families with them. Most of the workers will return to their mainland homes on weekends.

Step 1.   **Questions to analyzing your SIA project**

A. Based on information from project proponents, develop an age, gender, racial and ethic profile of the persons who will be introduced into the community as a result of the proposed action. Our example uses construction workers, but it could be tourists, students, new residents, or employees servicing the cruise ship industry.

Will the project introduce new groups into the community?
Yes ☐ No ☐; If Yes, complete Table 7.5; If No, go to Table 7.6.

B. Data to complete table 7.5 comes from basic population statistics and also may be obtained from local government data, census information and employment statistics. Local Heath Departments also collect and maintain information on vital statistics.

Table 7.5
Demographic Characteristics-Canadian Dream Example

	Your Community	Const. Wkrs	% + -	Butchart	Const. Wkrs/	% + -
% Under 35	____	____	____	45	100	+55
% Minority	____	____	____	10	30	+20
% Female	____	____	____	53	0	-53
% Ethnic/ Race	____	____	____	3	10 (Black)	+7

Step 2.   Enter significant results

If any of the differences in Table 7.5 are greater than ten percent, enter this information in Chapter 12 on page 138 and write your interpretation of the analysis below. Otherwise go on to the next chapter.

Interpret the results of your analysis for SIA #5

_____

_____

_____

_____

_____

*Remember, each of the Social Impact Assessment Variables is an **Indicator**! Research by social scientists has shown that a change in each of the social impact assessment variables is a clue to a possible social impact. Adding all the clues together will give you a good picture of likely future impacts.*

Summary of Chapter 7

Table 7.6 suggests which population SIA variables are likely to occur for each of the scenarios used in Chapter 7. Complete the table using the information you have obtained for the five population variables based on the <u>proposed action</u> you are assessing.

Table 7.6

Population Impact Assessment Variables	Your Community	ACME Waste Mgt (Siting)	Barn-Wall (Business)	Crestview Hospital (Closing)	Canadian Dream (Housing)
1. Population change.	_____	Possible	Possible	Yes	Yes
2. Influx or outflux of temporary workers.	_____	Yes	Yes	No	Yes
3. Presence of seasonal (leisure) residents.	_____	No	No	No	Yes
4. Relocation of individuals and families.	_____	Yes	No	No	No
5. Dissimilarity in age, gender, race or ethnic composition.	_____	Possible	Possible	No	Possible

*Remember, the purpose of the activities in **The Community Guide to Social Impact Assessment** is to provide an indicator as to the type and magnitude of likely social impacts as the result of a <u>proposed action</u>. Once a significant social impact has been identified, you must interpret the findings within the context of your assessment. For example, if 35 families must be relocated and most are older and long term residents, ask how will that move alter their lives? Will they experience stress? Will they be separated from long time friends and relatives? The **Guide** provides an indicator, but you must take it from there.*

Chapter 8. Community and Institutional Arrangements

How will your community and the institutions within it change due to the proposed project, policy change or new development?

The objective of this chapter is to measure social impacts to include community attitudes and perceptions, the formation of interest groups, the size of local government—to how the wage and occupational structure of the community will change as a result of the proposed action. All, however, have to do with the community and the institutions within which the people work!

SIA 6. Assessing the Formation of Attitudes toward the Project

Definition: By attitudes we mean the positive or negative feelings, beliefs or positions, expressed by residents in the community regarding the proposed project (or a policy change).

Instructions: **Why should we consider attitudes toward a <u>proposed action</u>?** While completing your SIA, you should be alert for clues on how persons in the impacted community see the <u>proposed action</u>. We call these *attitudes*. You do not have to be a sociologist to recognize that attitudes, both pro and con, begin to form among community members toward the proposed change starting the moment an announcement is made. Furthermore, an assessment of attitudes will provide information on the *climate* within the community that will prevail during the planning/decision stage and during both construction and operation. Public attitudes may be crucial in the political decision to proceed, whether changes in the project are necessary and to what degree mitigation measures are needed. Most change has both benefits and consequences—therefore, the assessor must understand both positive and negative attitudes.

When **Acme Waste Management** announced their plan to site a new landfill north of Arvana, Illinois, it seemed everyone had an opinion on the issue. From the very first day, opinions and attitudes began to form toward the proposed landfill. The local newspaper carried articles, a series of public hearings were held and a sociology class at state university studied attitudes toward the proposed landfill. All these information sources will help us assess the formation of attitudes toward the project.

Step 1. **Procedures to determine the presence of attitudes toward the project.**

A. Is information available on attitudes toward the project from articles and editorials in local or nearby newspapers expressing both pro and con views?

Yes ☐   No ☐

B. At public meetings, clubs and voluntary associations and formal hearings about the proposed project, have different views about the <u>proposed action</u> been voiced?

Yes ☐   No ☐

C. Have any representative surveys or public opinion polls been conducted in the community about the proposed project?

Yes ☐   No ☐

D. Have any informational websites, chat rooms, a facebook or electronic "townhalls" been set-up by project proponents, municipal and county planning offices or opposition groups?

Yes ☐   No ☐; If Yes, list them here:

_____

_____

_____

Step 2.   If the answer to any of the questions in Step 1 is **yes**, from newspapers, comments at public meetings and public opinion surveys—please complete Table 8.1 for your community. Otherwise, go on to SIA #7 on the next page.

Table 8.1
Attitudes Toward the Project

	Your Community	**Acme Waste Landfill**
Newspaper Articles and Letters to the Editor		
# Favorable	_____	5 (67%)
# Unfavorable	_____	3 (38%)
Comments at Public Meetings		
# Favorable	_____	12 (66%)
# Unfavorable	_____	6 (34%)
Letters from Citizens		
# Favorable	_____	30 (93%)
# Unfavorable	_____	2 (7%)
Representative Public Opinion Surveys		
% Favorable	_____	34%
% Unfavorable	_____	66%

Step 4.   **Enter Significant Results.**

If any results in Table 8.1 show at least 35% against the proposed project or change, enter these percentages in Chapter 12 on page 139.

Notes: summarize and interpret your findings for SIA #6

_____

_____

_____

_____

_____

_____

SIA 7. *Assessing Interest Group Activity*

Definition: Every community has formal and informal groups and organizations (sometimes called voluntary organizations) which may have an interest in the proposed change and may take a public stance one way or the other. Examples of interest groups, in the U.S., include the Farm Bureau, Chamber of Commerce's, service organizations such as the Rotary or the Lion's Club, environmental groups like the Sierra Club and the Audubon Society. Spontaneous, informal groups, such as the Concerned Citizens of Clark County may form for the purpose of supporting (or opposing) the proposed project (outside of the U.S. and Canada, these groups are referred to as non-governmental organizations [NGO's], or interested and affected parties).

Instructions: **Why is it important to know about interest group activity?** Interest groups and organizations are identifiable social forces active in the community that represent the views of their membership which either stand to gain or lose by the proposed action (or change in legislation or policy). Both their membership characteristics and attitudes toward the project should be understood and analyzed in the assessment process. Interest groups play an important role in shaping community responses and may help community leaders or benefit recipients during the mitigation/enhancement process (Chapter 13).

A consistent finding in SIA research literature is that community and neighborhood level interest groups always emerge, both for, as well as against, a proposed project. However, both formal and informal interest groups can also be valuable allies in strengthening project proposals. In the case of the Village of Arvana, two spontaneous citizen groups (Help End Landfill Pollution [HELP] and Citizens for A Safe Environment [CASE]) formed to oppose the landfill. However, the Chamber of Commerce and the Farm Bureau, both with large and influential memberships, supported the siting of the landfill because it was seen as safe, would be up-to-date and concentrate waste in one controlled location.

Step 1. Tabulate information about the community.

A.   As part of the scoping process outlined in Chapter 4, you as the social assessor compiled a list of "stakeholders" or "interested and affected parties." These persons and organizations represent a list of persons who have an interest in the outcome of the project. Many of the stakeholder groups will come from the immediate vicinity of the project. Include those in the tabulations for Table 8.2.

B.   Additional information to complete the Table 8.2 may be obtained from telephone listings, the library, local directories of civic and community organizations, petitions and a list of project sponsors. Local planning departments, and charitable, business and citizen organizations will be helpful in obtaining lists of voluntary organizations in your community. You may limit the number of interest groups contacted for this variable depending on those interested in the proposed action.

Caution: Generally, leaders, or the official spokesperson, reflect the views of the membership they represent or they would not be in position of responsibility. However, as the social assessor, be alert for situations where leaders do not represent followers or even if there are followers. The Superintendent of Olympia National Park in the U.S. State of Washington wanted to remove an old dam that was blocking salmon runs on the Elwha River. The only opposition was a "Save the Dam" citizen group complete with website and a vocal leader. He turned out to be the only member of that "citizen group."

Step 2. Procedures for determining interest group activity. Complete Table 8.2 for your assessment project. The yellow pages of the phone book or electronic directories may be helpful—look, for example, under: Human and Social Services, Professional and Business Clubs, Youth and Senior Organizations, Environmental, Fraternal and Foundations, Labor and Women's Organizations, Education and Health, and Homeowners' Associations.

Table 8.2
Interest Group Activity

	Your Community	Acme Waste Landfill
Groups and Organizations		
Number Favorable	_____	3
Number Unfavorable	_____	17
% Groups Unfavorable	_____	85%
Estimated membership of groups and organizations		
Number Favorable	_____	523
Number Unfavorable	_____	345
% Membership Unfavorable	_____	40%

Step 3. Enter Significant Results. If your analysis shows that more than 25 percent of the organizations and groups and/or the persons in them oppose the proposed action, enter the information from Table 8.2 in Chapter 12 on page 139, otherwise, go to SIA #8. However, remember that formal and informal interest groups may be helpful during the mitigation, enhancement and monitoring stages.

Write the results of your analysis for SIA #7

_____

_____

_____

_____

_____

_____

SIA 8. Assessing Alteration in the Size and Structure of Local Government

Definition: We here mean a change (plus or minus) in the number and type of positions necessary to run local government activities as a result of the proposed project. This SIA variable applies to the operation/maintenance or decommissioning/closing phase of a project and should not be confused with change in community infrastructure needs (SIA #26) as outlined in Chapter 11. SIA #8 measures change in the size and occupational composition of local government staff.

Instructions: **Why do we need to know about changes in the size and structure of local government?** Changes in the size and composition of local government generally occur if the project results in an increase or decrease in the demand (or need) for local government services. For example, existing funding and staffing levels may be inadequate to meet demands for municipal and county level planning, infrastructure development and utility services, tax collection, and other types of government support due to project needs. While community leaders may provide the needed initiative, enhancing project benefits is generally the result of a competent, well paid professional staff able to follow through on details.

Local government may begin to operate more formally and bureaucratically as the volume and complexity of its responsibilities increase. For example, as the size of the population increases, local governments must expand community services. Unless personnel and organizational changes are anticipated, local government may not be able to cope and the benefits of a project may be lost. Staff may be so overwhelmed or so politically obligated, that decisions are *not* made to protect and enhance all persons and amenities in the community. As local government becomes more professional and formal, its special relationship with long term residents could be altered.

As an example, the population of the Island Municipality and Village of Butchart will increase dramatically as a result of the **Canadian Dream Residential Development** (up 129%). To meet the needs of new residents the size and structure of municipal government will also increase. The social impact assessment of the **Canadian Dream** development raised two important questions. First, were the new revenues generated by the project sufficient to cover the costs of more government services? Second, was the municipal staff sufficiently skilled to deal with the complexities of monitoring a major residential development? If not, would they be able to recruit government workers skilled, for example, in the complexities of tertiary sewage treatment or procedures for minimizing surface water runoff? "Skill level" might include financial or technical expertise and, for example, dispute resolution and organizational administration.

Step 1. **Determine change in size of government.**

A. In Table 8.3, enter the number of full-time equivalent persons presently employed by the jurisdiction having supervisory or regulatory responsibility for the proposed action who are **not** elected officials.

B. If the local government under study does not have full time persons in these positions, but contracts for these services, indicate the approximate full-time equivalent positions contracted for village/ city/ shire/ municipal activities.

Table 8.3 Changes in Local Government

Position	Your Comm. Present	Your Comm. With Project	Variance (+/-)	Butchart Present	Can. Dream Project	Variance (+/-)
Judicial/Legal	___	___	___	.25	1.0	-.75
Engineers	___	___	___	--	0.5	-0.5
Admin./ Manager	___	___	___	--	1.0	-1.0
Clerical	___	___	___	1.0	1.0	0.0
Inspectors	___	___	___	1.0	2.0	-1.0
Planning	___	___	___	--	1.0	-1.0
Public Works	___	___	___	1.0	3.0	-2.0
Assessors/Finance	___	___	___	2.0	3.5	-1.5
Regulatory	___	___	___	___	1.0	-1.0
Totals	....	....	....	5.25	14.0	**-8.75**

Step 2. **Interpretation of Results**

Data in Table 8.3 may be interpreted two ways. First, is the experiece level present in local government able to handle expanded government responsibilities (examples are additional governmental supervision required for the implementation of environmental directives, compliance with state, provincial and federal regulations or local building codes designed to minimize environmental damage)? A second interpretation is the change in the actual number of employees as a percentage of present employees.

Step 3. If the projected increase in the total number of positions is greater than three (3), enter in Chapter 12 on page 140; otherwise go to SIA #9. The following sites have information on standards for number of government employees on a per 1,000 population basis :

http://www.naco.org/ or www.associationofcities.org/ or www.nic.org/

SIA 9. Assessing the Presence of Planning and Zoning Activity

Definition: SIA #9 refers to the presence (or absence) of legal mandates for development, planning, zoning and/or land use regulations within the local township, municipality, village, county, state or provincial government that has jurisdiction within the proposed project area.

Instructions: **Why is planning and zoning important?** If planning and zoning safeguards as well as the institutions and personnel to implement them are ***not*** present in your community they may have to be legislated. Coping with population or infrastructure growth or decline will be easier if planning, zoning, or special tax and service districts are in place in the impact area prior to the proposed development or policy change. For example, very few U.S. counties have completed a county-wide comprehensive plan (to include land use controls), and therefore may not have established zoning or subdivision ordinances or the available staff to anticipate the problems and benefits that may result from a proposed development.

> "Farmers and other rural landowners have resisted zoning and growth management plans because they do not (did not) want anyone to tell them what to do with their land (private property rights). Now they are discovering that with no zoning in place, others are bringing undesirable development to their communities: landfills, sub-standard housing and polluting industries, to name a few."

For example, in the community where the **Canadian Dream** residential development was proposed, municipal leaders resisted the implementation of planning because Butchart was small and the population had been relatively stable. With the coming of this major development, it was difficult to anticipate future needs or to minimize environment damage because controls were not in place at the time the development was proposed. As a result, all residents of the Island Municipality had to pay increased taxes for new roads, as well as new water and tertiary sewage systems. The lack of environmental safeguards led to silted streams and erosion from roads and construction.

Step 1. Obtain data from municipal, city, village, or county records to determine the presence or absence of each level of planning and zoning activity, for the political jurisdictions in your project area.

Enter the information on Table 8.4 for your SIA project.

Table 8.4
Planning and Zoning

Planning and Zoning Component	Your Community Currently		Canadian Dream Currently	
	Yes	No	Yes	No
Comprehensive Plan	_____	_____		X
Growth Management Act	_____	_____		X
Zoning Laws	_____	_____		X
Spot Zoning Allowed	_____	_____	X	
Subdivision Ordinances	_____	_____		X
Building Codes	_____	_____		X
Critical Areas Ordnances	_____	_____		X
Costal Zone Regulations	_____	_____		X
Environmental Regulations	_____	_____		X
Wetlands Restrictions	_____	_____		X
Certified Planner (Staff or Consultant)	_____	_____		X
Other_____	_____	_____		

Step 2.   **Enter Significant Results.**

If you answered **NO** to any of the questions on planning and zoning in Table 8.4, enter the total number in this space _____ and the number and type in Chapter 12 on page 141.

☞ Obtain a map showing the zoning and land use regulations (if any) in the social impact assessment area.

Comment on the results of your analysis for SIA #9

_____

_____

_____

SIA 10. Assessing Industrial Diversification

Definition: Industrial diversification refers to the number and variety of private sector industries (manufacturers, retailers, services, etc.) within the proposed project area.

Instructions: **Why is industrial diversity important to a community?** One of the goals of community development is to diversify the industrial and service sectors in the local economy; both directly through the presence of new employers and indirectly through the local sale of equipment, supplies and services produced by other industries and also through goods and services produced by its employees. If, as a result of the proposed action, the purchase of goods and services remain within the community, other sectors of the community can be expected to grow.

Research has shown that the capacity to diversify must be present if the benefits of development are to remain within the community. Also, if the benefits of the project are temporary, induced diversification may not lend stability to the local economy, since it depends solely on the project as the major consumer. If the local economy is diverse, it will be better able to absorb the impact event and benefit. As an example, Rantoul, Illinois is seeking replacements for Chanute Air Base which closed in 1993. The community is seeking a diverse array of public and private sector organizations, i.e., "more than one egg to fill the basket." Development could lead to diversification, but research has shown that industrial and infrastructure capacity has to be present for the community to capitalize on the benefits. If a diversified economy and other amenities are present, it is easier to attract new employers.

> "There are two issues in diversification—will it help to survive change and will it lead to even more industrial diversification?"

Historically, Darnell has been a trade center for the surrounding small towns and the agricultural community. The small manufacturing plants that were there have left the community. The number of farms has declined and the farm implement and feed stores may leave if the trend continues. The addition of **Barn-Wall** has expanded the retail trade area, but has produced few spin-off firms. **Barn-Wall** has undercut the price of the Darnell merchants and most of these shops must now close. However, since **Barn-Wall** is in the sales (retail trade) sector, the business activity is consistent with the historical focus of the community.

Step 1. **A procedure for determining industrial diversification.**

Complete Table 8.5 using data obtained from a recent county or municipal business census or reports of tax receipts, payrolls and property tax.
For an example list of the different categories of public and private sectors organizations and business go to:
　http://www.census.gov/econ/census02/guide/

Table 8.5 Industrial Diversification

Type of Firm or Establishment	Number Present	Your Community with Project	Num. +/-	Darnell Present	Darnell with Project	Num. +/-
Agric, Forestry, Mining	_____	_____	___	6	6	0
Construction	_____	_____	___	2	3	+1.0
Manufacturing	_____	_____	___	3	3	0
Transportation and Public Utilities	_____	_____	___	1	1	--
Wholesale Trade	_____	_____	___	1	2	+1.0
Retail Trade	_____	_____	___	10	15	+5.0
Finance, Insurance, Real Estate, Information	_____	_____	___	5	6	+1.0
Accommodations, Food Service	_____	_____	___	10	11	+1.0
General Services	_____	_____	___	2	3	+1.0
Health Care Organizations	_____	_____	___	1	1	--
Educational Org.	_____	_____	___	3	3	0
State and Local Gov. Administration.	_____	_____	___	2	2	--
Total Firms and Establishments	_____	_____	___	46	56	+10.0

Step 2.   **Evaluating Significant Results.** If the total number of firms is large and/or a diverse industrial profile is present, the community will be in a better position to receive the benefits of the proposed development. However, if it is a *one horse* or *one industry* town, you need to explain in detail how the proposed action will alter the mix of businesses and industries.

Step 3.   Check this box ☐ if industrial diversity will **not** increase with the proposed development. In addition, enter the totals above in Chapter 12, page 141.

SIA 11. Assessing the Presence of Living/Family Wage Levels

Definition: A living/family wage refers to the amount of money required for the average family of four to live above the poverty line in the community/region or country where the proposed change is located.

Instruction: SIA #11 is the first in a series of four variables which uses information about jobs and the numbers of persons who are unemployed in the community. Many projects or policy changes proudly point to the number of future jobs created if approval is given. Conversely, if a plant is closed or an agency consolidates, we need to know the number of jobs lost. But we must ask what kinds of jobs are lost? Are they minimum wage positions, which, for example, in the United States in 2007 was $5.15 an hour? Would that wage be high enough to support a family of four when only one person was employed? What is included in a living/family wage? The consumer price index is a measure of what it costs to meet basic necessities: food, housing, clothing, healthcare, transportation, utilities, and miscellaneous.

Each year a poverty threshold is established--generally between 40 and 45 percent of the median family income of the area. In the U.S., the Census Bureau provides estimates of median family income for each geographical area. The Bureau of Labor Statistics updates estimates on the cost of living and the number of unemployed in each part of the country on a quarterly basis.

http://www.bls.gov/or www.census.gov/
www.bls.gov/oes/2001/oes_alph.htm

Step 1   **Calculating the living /family wage for your community:**

Enter median family income for your area _____ x 43%

= $_____ Poverty Level.

Example: the U.S. median income in 2004 was about $42,000 x 43% = approximately $18,100 for a family of four to be above the poverty level.

Enter hourly wage for each job_____ x 2000 hours per year

= _____ yearly family income for each job classification.

Example: Security guards make $7.26 per hour x 2000 hours for a yearly family income of $14,520.

Example: The family wage earner in the U.S. needed to make $9.05 per hour in 2004 for a yearly family income above the poverty level. Examples of the average hourly wages for hundreds of U.S. occupations may be found at:
www.bls.gov/oes/2001/oes_alph.htm

Step 2. **Obtain a profile of the positions from the project proponent, or if your project is a closure, the present list of employees by job classification.**

Enter the number in each job category shown in Table 8.6. Also, enter the number of positions in the study community occupying each of the present job descriptions. You should change the occupational listings in Table 8.6 to fit the project you are assessing.

Step 3. **Entering Significant Results**

Is the number of Living/Family level jobs created (or lost), greater than 50% of the total number for all job categories? (Divide Living/Family level jobs by total number of new or lost jobs.)
Yes ☐   No ☐

Do part-time jobs make up for more than 25% of the positions?
Yes ☐   No ☐

If you answered **No** to the first question and/or **Yes** to the second, enter your data from Table 8.6 in Chapter 12, page 142.

In the example shown in Table 8.6, only eight (8) of the new positions paid enough to allow a family of four to live above the poverty level and most of the jobs were less than full-time.

Interpret the results of your analysis for SIA #11

_____

_____

_____

_____

_____

_____

_____

_____

Table 8.6 Living/Family Wage

Name of Business or Employer _____

(Barn-Wall is our example.)

Job Description[a]	Project Job Numbers	Hourly Wage	Number Above Poverty	Number Part-Time	Project Job Numbers	Hourly Wage	Number Above Poverty	Number Part-Time
Farm/Forest/Mine Operators					--	--	--	--
Farm/Forest/Mine Workers					--	--	--	--
Professional/Technical					1	14.00	1	0
Managers/Proprietors					3	12.75	3	0
Clerical/Sales					70	6.50	0	40
Production/Foreman					4	9.50	4	1
Operative/Drivers					4	8.50	0	1
Service Occupations					10	8.00	0	6
Laborers/Food service					4	6.50	0	2
Maids/Janitors					6	5.95	0	6
Construction/Installation					2	7.50	0	0
TOTALS	____	____ (Median)	____	____	**104**	**6.50** (Median)	**8** (7.7%)	**56** (54%)

[a] For easier assessment, adjust the occupational categories to fit your country and eliminate categories that do not apply. The U.S. Census uses the broad categories of management, business and financial operations; professional and related occupations; service occupations; sales and office occupations; natural resources, construction and maintenance (includes farming, fishing and forestry); and production, transportation, and material moving. The numbers were current at the time of the assessment.

SIA 12. Assessing Enhanced Economic Inequities

Definition: Enhanced Economic Inequities refers to the degree to which employment opportunities of the proposed project or development match the job skills of the unemployed in the project area.

Instructions: **Why should we look at potential economic inequities?** Project justification often hinges on the expectation that the proposed action will create jobs, especially for those currently unemployed. SIA variable #12 examines the match between jobs available from the project and the job skills of the locally unemployed. A new project employing only highly skilled computer programmers may raise the overall income level of your community, but will not help unemployed factory or farm workers. In fact, as pointed out later in this chapter, it might actually contribute to greater inequity. Again, we are asking the question..."what type of jobs and who gets them?"

Step 1. **Procedures for checking on possible economic inequities.**

A. In the previous SIA variable (#11), you gathered information about the wage scale for added (or lost) jobs due to the project. Now we need information on the unemployed. Some of these data will be available from the local unemployment office as well as monthly payroll reports. Most U.S. states and Canadian provinces have a Bureau of Labor Statistics and unemployment (economic security) offices are located in most municipalities. In this portion of the SIA we are looking for a match between the types of employment opportunities available from the proposed project and the job skills of the unemployed persons in the community.

B. Using data on job titles or a labor force profile, complete Table 8.7 on the unemployed within the project area.

C. Next, enter the number of jobs created by the proposed project based on data from Table 8.6. Assuming all project jobs will go to the unemployed in your community, calculate the actual reduction in numbers of unemployed. For the **Barn-Wall** example, 49 of the 104 new positions matched the job skills of the unemployed, resulting in an 18% reduction in unemployment.

Step 2. **Entering Significant Results.**

Do the job opportunities available from the proposed project reduce or increase overall unemployment by 10% for the sum of all job categories? (divide change by number unemployed)

Yes ☐   No ☐   If Yes, enter the job category and percent change from Table 8.7 in Chapter 12, page 143.

Table 8.7 Enhanced Economic Inequities

Job Category	Your Community			Barn-Wall Store		
	Number Unemployed	Project Job Number	Projected Number unemployed	Current Number unemployed	Employee Numbers	Projected Number unemployed
Farm/Forest/Mine Operators	___	___	|	--	--	--
Farm/Forest/Mine Workers	___	___	|	--	--	--
Professional/Technical	___	___	|	10	1	9
Managers/Proprietors	___	___	|	25	3	22
Clerical/Sales	___	___	|	15	70	--
Craftsman/Foreman	___	___	|	30	4	26
Operatives/Drivers	___	___	|	50	4	46
Service Occupations	___	___	|	25	10	15
Laborers/Food Service	___	___	|	50	4	46
Maids/Janitors	___	___	|	20	6	14
Construction/Installation	___	___	|	40	2	38
Totals Unemployment and New Jobs	___		|	265	104	216
Percent Change (+ or -)	+ or -					-18%

See notes on occupational categories on Table 8.6

SIA 13. Assessing Change in Employment Equity of Minority Groups

Definition: By employment equity for minorities, we mean the degree to which job opportunities of the proposed project match the job skills of the unemployed, disadvantaged and minority groups to include low-income, younger persons, ethnic and racial minorities as well as women.

Instructions: **Why do we need to consider the employment opportunities of minority persons?** Jobs resulting from new or expanded project development are *not* equitably distributed among unemployed community members on the basis of geography, ethnic origin, gender and/or race. When balancing the combined negative impacts (costs) and positive impacts (benefits), be alert for mismatches. You may uncover situations where one category of the population is significantly benefiting, while others will be harmed in many different ways by the proposed project.

> "…will the unemployed and underemployed benefit from new job opportunities or will competition increase among those presently employed?"

While working through this *Guide* be aware that the project may indirectly enhance or hinder social equity in the impacted community. (We hope all projects enhance equity.) This step in the analysis utilizes some of the same information obtained for SIA #12 in Table 8.7 (enhanced economic inequities) but is designed to determine if job benefits will be extended to specific segments of the unemployed or indigenous (native) populations who might otherwise not have employment opportunities.

In the **Barn-Wall** example, 145 of the unemployed persons in the study area were minorities. If all of the available job categories were matched with the unemployed, it would reduce minority employment by 17 percent. However, in the town of Darnell few of the job skills of the minorities (except for females) matched the new jobs available at the **Barn-Wall** store.

In analyzing the community of Darnell, we found the unemployed to be previous store owners, craftsman, machine operators and truck drivers (almost all male) many whom worked in the manufacturing plants that had closed down. Most of the jobs available at **Barn-Wall** were minimum wage entry positions for sales clerks, cashiers, stockers, maids, janitors, and security guards. A few management positions were available, but most of these went to trainees brought in from the outside by the **Barn-Wall** organization.

In the **Barn-Wall** example, we found that most occupational opportunities accrue to sales personnel and janitors. Both jobs require little in the way of skilled training. As we found in the case of industrial diversification, the **Barn-Wall** store will not create high paid living/family wage opportunities. However, the new store does fit within the retail trade focus of the community.

Step 1.   **Procedure to check for project employment opportunities for minorities.**

A. List categories of minorities in your assessment community

_____   _____

_____   _____

B. From **SIA #12** you obtained information about jobs and the numbers of persons unemployed for each of the major occupational categories for the study community—enter those in Table 8.8.

C. Next, obtain a list of the job titles of the unemployed minorities in your study area. Most of these data will be available from the local office of unemployment and monthly payroll reports. For example, in Illinois, these data come from the Bureau of Economic Analysis. However, considerable detective work may be necessary to find details on these job titles and the local unemployment office will be the best source.

D. Using data on job titles obtained from the project proponent and the job titles of unemployed minorities, complete Table 8.8 for your study area.

Find the website for unemployment data for your municipality, shire or county and list it here:

_____

Step 2.   **Interpreting Results**

In this portion of the analysis you are looking for a match between employment opportunities available from the proposed project and the job skills of unemployed minorities.

Do the job categories available from the proposed project match the job titles of **minorities** unemployed in the community? Yes ☐   No ☐

If Yes, what percent _____?

Step 3.   **Enter Significant Results.** If No, the lack of employment opportunities for minorities could be a significant social impact, now transfer your information from Table 8.8 to Chapter 12, page 144.

Table 8.8 Employment of Minorities

Job Category	Your Community			Barn-Wall Store		
	Current Minorities unemployed	Project Job Number	Projected Minorities unemployed	Current Minorities unemployed	Employee Numbers	Projected Minorities unemployed
Farm/Forest/Mine Operators				--	--	--
Farm/Forest/Mine Workers				25	--	25
Professional/Technical				--	1	--
Managers/Proprietors				--	3	--
Clerical/Sales				5	70	--
Craftsman/Foreman				20	4	16
Operatives/Drivers				30	4	26
Service Occupations				20	10	10
Laborers/Food Service				10	4	6
Maids/Janitors				15	6	9
Construction/Installation				20	2	18
Total Minority Unemployment and New Jobs				145	104	110
Percent Change(+ or -)		+ or -...			-17%	

SIA 14. Assessing Changing Occupational Opportunities

Definition: By changing occupational opportunities, we mean the degree to which the proposed project or development will alter the occupational profile of the impacted community.

Instructions: **What do we need to know about changing occupational opportunities?** The creation of new job opportunities means that local labor may be drawn from the unemployed, those not previously considered part of the labor force or they may be recruited from those presently employed. Housewives may become maids and service workers which is an example of project-induced growth. The resulting change in occupational opportunities may lead to changes in family income, in family roles and even major life style changes for persons receiving the new positions. Those not participating in the new occupational opportunities may also find their relative situation changing. The different types of jobs available in the community may mean a requirement for a different set of skills, which could attract new members to a community and may bring about social conflict.

> " As resource dependent communities decline we ask the questions: Can mill workers become computer programmers?; can loggers become chamber maids; can fishermen become Blackjack dealers?…probably not in the same generation."

Other indirect effects of increased employment opportunities may include the retention of young adults in the community who otherwise might have left. Project development may also discourage local youths from acquiring higher education levels and remain in non-skilled positions. For example, the transformation from a timber-dependent community to a tourist service community could mean jobs for women (as maids) and none for men who previously worked as loggers.

In the case of **Barn-Wall,** in the community of Darnell, the unemployed were store owners, craftsmen (generally male) and machine operators and truck drivers who had worked in the manufacturing plants that were now closed. Most of the jobs available at **Barn-Wall** are minimum wage entry positions for sales clerks, cashiers, stockers and janitors. A few management trainee positions were available, but most of these went to trainees in the **Barn-Wall** organization. We found some significant changes. As shown in Table 8.9, the percentage of sales/cashier positions increased by 37%. Janitorial positions increased substantially.

Step 1. **Data to analyze changing occupational opportunities.**

A. To analyze the SIA variable on changing occupational opportunities you need the entire occupational profile for your community. Use the same data sources as for the previous three SIA variables. To obtain an occupational profile by geographical area within the U.S., go to http://www.census.gov/geo/www/tiger/index.html These same occupational categories will also be used for SIA #16 in Chapter 9.

B. Utilizing data on job titles complete Table 8.9 for your community.

C. There are two ways to interpret the information in Table 8.9. In SIA #14 we are looking for the types of jobs which will experience project related growth. In SIA #17 (next chapter) we will use the same information to look for change in social classes.

D. Do the job categories available from the proposed project significantly increase or decrease more than 10 percent for any job classification for your community? Yes ☐ No ☐.

If Yes, write in Chapter 12 on page 145 those occupational classifications where an increase or decrease is greater than 10%.

Step 2. **Interpretation.** In this portion of the social impact assessment you are looking for similarities/dissimilarities between the types of employment opportunities available from the proposed project and the occupational array of the presently employed persons in the impact community.

Interpret the results of your analysis for SIA #14

_____

_____

_____

_____

_____

_____

_____

Table 8.9
Changes in Occupational Opportunities

Occupational Description	Your Community			Barn-Wall Store		
	Current Number employed	Project Job Numbers	Percent Change (+ or -)	Current Number employed	Project Job Numbers	Percent Change (+/-)
Farm/Forest/Mine Operator	___	___	___	380	--	0
Farm/Forest/Mine Worker	___	___	___	220	--	0
Professional/Technical	___	___	___	40	1	+2
Managers/Proprietors	___	___	___	49	3	+6
Clerical/Sales	___	___	___	190	70	+37
Production/Foreman	___	___	___	85	4	+5
Operatives/Drivers	___	___	___	64	4	+6
Service Occupations	___	___	___	106	10	+9
Laborers/Food Service	___	___	___	45	4	+9
Maids/Janitors	___	___	___	28	6	+21
Construction/Installation	___	___	___	84	2	+2
Totals and Percent Change	( )	( )	( )	1,291	104	+ 8.1%

Summary of Chapter 8 Table 8.10 shows which community and institutional changes are likely to occur for each of the examples used in this book. Using the illustrations as guidelines complete Table 8.10 using the information you have obtained for the nine-community and institutional social impact assessment variables.

Table 8.10 Summary of SIA Variables for Community and Institutional Arrangements

Community/Institutional SIA Variables	Your Community	Acme Waste Mgt. (Siting)	Barn-Wall (Business)	Crestview Hospital (Closing)	Canadian Dream (Housing)
6. Formation of attitudes toward the project...	___	Yes	Yes	Possible	Possible
7. Interest group activity...	___	Yes	Possible	Possible	Possible
8. Alteration in size and structure of local government...	___	Unlikely	Unlikely	Possible	Yes
9. Presence of planning and zoning activity...	___	Yes	Yes	No	Yes
10. Industrial diversification...	___	Yes	Yes	Yes	Yes
11. Living/Family Wage	___	Yes	Less	Loss	Yes
12. Enhanced economic inequities...	___	Likely	Possible	Yes	Unlikely
13. Change in employment equity of minority groups...	___	Likely	Unlikely	Likely	Unlikely
14. Changing occupational opportunities...	___	Yes	Yes	Yes	Likely

Chapter 9.   Communities in Transition

How will the proposed project or policy change alter existing social arrangements in your community? Will there be conflict among local residents and newcomers or even outsiders? If yes, how will these events change the image residents have of their community?

You must now address the question of how the proposed action will alter the major individual, organizational, institutional, social class and power structure relationships within the community. Most of the change in the dynamics of community relations will be due to the arrival (or departure) of a new government agency or private sector organization, the introduction of new classes of persons or even a change in the commercial focus of the community. Most communities are in transition, but development events exacerbate the change.

The objectives of this chapter are:

1. To assess the presence and influence of an outside agency;

2. To determine the level of cooperation among public and private sector agencies and organizations in your community;

3. To assess the influence of the proposed action on social classes and occupational categories;

4. To assess changes in the commercial and industrial focus in the community and;

5. To assess the impact of weekend residents on community relationships.

➡

SIA 15. Assessing the Presence of an Outside Agency

Definition: By presence of an outside agency we mean the taking up of permanent residency (or departure) in the project (impact) area of a government agency or private sector business or industry (the project operator or proponent), which has not previously been in the community and whose management and control (decision-making) comes from outside the area.

Instructions: **Why is it important?** An outside agency or organization may make decisions affecting local communities which are not responsive to local needs and priorities. Decisions which are not in line with local interest may prove to be a major source of dissatisfaction among community, county and municipality residents. The presence of a new employer could significantly alter existing social relationships and the local community power structure depending upon the occupational and income levels of the arriving employees.

Step 1.   **An Example**

> The proposal by the U.S. National Park Service to re-introduce wolves to Olympic National Park was based on the need for predator control. The locals were furious because they were not consulted during the decision-making process.

The U.S. Army Corps of Engineers is an example of an outside agency. Decisions on the management of flood control reservoirs, such as Lake Shelbyville (in central Illinois, U.S.), are made in accordance with procedures developed in St. Louis, Missouri and Washington, D.C. The resident lake manager, while sympathetic to local interests and needs, must follow orders from superiors. The decision to nominate Queensland's (Australia) northern tropical rainforests for World Heritage listing was made on the basis of national interests for eco-system preservation and not on the social impacts it would have on the local logging community. Private sector organizations such as Toyota and Honda open and close plants based on bottom line financial decisions and not on how a closing would alter the social class and occupational structure of the host community. The key issue is who makes the decisions and will the local community have any say.

The residents of Rural County have heard the presentation of **Acme Waste** and the many promises and benefits for the municipality of Arvana, if the landfill is sited next to their community. However, community residents also know that corporate headquarters are in Chicago, Illinois and that management will change, particularly during the 30 year life of the landfill. Will **Acme Waste** always be a "good neighbor" as portrayed by the site negotiator, or will problems arise and the community be left holding a bag of serious environmental problems when the landfill closes?

Step 2.   **Determining the Presence of an Outside Agency.**

A. Does the proposed project mean the arrival or departure of public agencies or private sector industry or business (departure, if a project is being decommissioned) in your community?

Yes ☐   No ☐

If No, go on to SIA #16. As a help in identification, remember that during scoping in Chapter 4 you identified key stakeholders and in SIA #7, you listed interest groups.

If you checked **Yes** above, list any *new* government or private sector agencies, businesses or industries that are coming to the community.

1.

_____

2.

_____

3.

_____

Table 9.1 Presence of Outside Agency

	Your Community	**Acme Waste**
Will an outside government agency or private sector organization come into or leave your community as a result of the <u>proposed action</u>?	_____	Yes

Step 3.   **Enter Significant Results**

If the answer to the question is a yes, community leaders and citizens may experience conflict with the new agencies and organizations, particularly if decisions are made outside the area. If any government agency or private sector organization is leaving, the community may experience a leadership void depending upon the amount of community leadership and involvement of the persons leaving. Enter the results from table 9.1 in Chapter 12 on page 146.

Interpret the results of your analysis for SIA #15

_____

_____

SIA 16. Determining the Level of Inter-Organizational Cooperation

Definition: The level of inter-organizational and governmental cooperation refers to the degree to which regulatory, planning and proponent organizations and agencies are able to work together and share common goals and policies. This variable requires looking at separate agencies at the same level, e.g., planning and public works at the local level or combinations at different levels, federal, provincial, state, and municipal. Legal jurisdiction or substantial financial interests are tests of involvement.

Instructions: To fully realize the benefits of a project or policy change, the proponent, the regulatory agency, the relevant planning organizations as well as the elected/appointed political bodies must to be able to work together toward common goals. Several steps are required of the assessor who must identify each organization and their respective roles in the decision/planning process. Private citizens, organizations and institutions each have goals and shared values. The same can be said of organizations that operate for the benefit of owners or shareholders.

> "Lack of communication among *stakeholders* is the biggest obstacle to understanding and dealing with the social consequences of policy decisions."
>
> Robin Dexter, Whatcom County, Washington

Actions undertaken in one area by a single agency may produce significant consequences in another location or even undermine the decisions of a separate agency within the same government. The Department of Lands may approve clear cutting on the upper reaches of a stream, which would destroy downstream attempts to improve fish habitat by the Department of Fish and Wildlife. The Public Works department may disapprove a **Barn-Wall** store because of storm water run-off while the finance department approves the project for the added tax revenues. A simple lack of communication among organizations and individuals is frequently the hidden source of failure to mitigate for the impact of other SIA variables.

For example, the Gateway Pacific Coal Terminal project described in 📖 *Concepts* Chapter 15, requires approvals from the planning department and a water district at the county level. The Departments of Ecology and Natural Resources at the State of Washington level as well as the Bellingham Port Authority which operates with State approval. At the Federal level, the U.S. Army Corps of Engineers must give the final approval, but not before negotiating with the Lummi Nation which has traditional fishing rights in the proposed project area.

Step 1. **Write here the decision(s) or proposed action to be made from Activity 4.2 in the first part of scoping.**

_____

_____

Step 2.   Data to determine the number and types of governmental organizations
               and agencies begins with the listing of key stakeholders identified during
               the scoping process and listed in Table 4.4. In addition look at all levels of
               government, including Aboriginal or First Nations, which would be
               required to either approve or review (be consulted) the proposed action
               and write these numbers in Table 9.2.

Table 9.2 Inter-organizational Cooperation

Level	Your Community		Canadian Dream	
	Approvals Required	Consultations Required	Approvals Required	Consultations Required
International	_____	_____	--	--
Federal	_____	_____	1	1
Aboriginal-First Nations	_____	_____	1	--
Provincial/State	_____	_____	1	2
Municipal/County	_____	_____	4	--
Village/Shire	_____	_____	4	--
Private Sector (Proponent)	_____	_____	1	1
TOTALS	_____	_____	12	4

Step 3.   **Enter significant results.** If the number of approvals is greater than four
               (4), successful cooperation will be limited. As a general rule the SIA
               practitioner should anticipate cooperation on problem solving in
               proportion to the number and size of the agencies and governmental units
               with authority and in proportion to the time frame and size of the project.
               Write the totals from Table 9.2 in Chapter 12, page 146.

Step 4.   Based on your experience in the impacted community and from
               discussions with citizens, planners and elected officials as well as
               proponents of similar projects, **rate the level of inter-organizational
               cooperation in the impact community:**

               Low ☐   OK ☐   High ☐

SIA 17. Assessing the Introduction of New Social Classes

Definition: By new social classes we mean the appearance (or disappearance) of a group of people that either expand an existing social class or establish a new social class (based on education and income levels, occupation or lifestyle) in the community as a result of the proposed action.

Instructions: **Why is it important to learn about new social classes?** The appearance in your community (or departure) of a group of people who, because of their education, income and/or occupation, have a different lifestyle than those of most long-term residents, may change the political and power relationships within the impact community. Social class characteristics may affect how the newcomers perceive the community and how the community perceives the newcomers. Differences may hinder acceptance and integration. The social class of newcomers may also affect their degree of involvement in community organizations and activities. There may also be disruption of traditional power structures as newcomers gain political control, thus exacerbating resentment among long-term residents in the impacted community.

Loss of key social class groupings can leave a leadership void. SIA research on the closing of military facilities in the U.S. during the 80s and 90s found that non-commissioned officers provided much of the leadership for such civic and youth groups as scouts, athletic leagues, Kiwanis, churches and community service organizations. Members of local labor unions provide leadership and facilities for youth groups—so when a plant closes, that leadership class is gone. In the U.S. Pacific Northwest, the staffs of the U.S. Forest Service ranger districts were cut when timber harvests declined. These professionals left a void in the volunteer leadership for timber-dependent communities.

When the **Canadian Dream** residential development is fully occupied, Island Municipality, and the nearby town of Butchart, will have changed. Long-term residents are likely to say that—*these people are not like us at all, they dress funny, ask if wine is available, want to know why we don't have nice restaurants, and a place where they can get a Mercedes repaired.* In short, Island Municipality has a new social class, with different values, expectations and life style. We continue with **Barn-Wall** as an example.

Table 9.3 Changes in Social Classes

Job Category	Your Community			Present Percent Employed	Barn-Wall Store	
	Present Percent Employed	Percent Employed w/wo Project	Percent Change (+ or -)		Percent Employed w/wo Project	Percent Change (+ or -)
Farm/Forest/Mine Operators	___	___	___	29	27	-2
Farm/Forest/Mine Workers	___	___	___	17	16	-1
Professional/ Technical	___	___	___	3	3	--
Managers/Proprietors	___	___	___	4	4	--
Clerical/Sales	___	___	___	15	19	+4
Craftsman/Foreman	___	___	___	7	6	-1
Operatives/Drivers	___	___	___	5	5	--
Service Occupations	___	___	___	8	8	--
Laborers/Food Service	___	___	___	4	4	--
Maids/Janitors	___	___	___	2	2	--
Construction/ Installation	___	___	___	6	6	--
TOTALS	100	100		100	100	0%

Step 1.　**Determining changes in social classes.**

A.　In Chapter 8, SIA #14, you developed an occupational profile for the community by obtaining information on the classification and numbers of jobs which might be added (or subtracted) as a result of the proposed project or policy change.

B.　Using the information from Table 8.9, calculate the percent of the total employed for each job category and enter in the first column labeled *Percent Employed* in Table 9.3.

C.　Next add the present and projected numbers for each job category and calculate a new percent for each classification. Enter this percent under the second column labeled *Percent employed w/wo (with or without) project.*

D.　In the next column under *change* enter the percentage increased or decreased for each job classification.

Step 2.　**Enter Significant Results**. If the total percentage change in any of the job classifications is greater than 5%, you have a significant change in the numbers of persons in a specific occupational category. Therefore, the proposed action has the potential for a change in the community social class structure depending upon the types of occupations in which the differences will occur. Write the significant information from Table 9.3 in Table 9.4 and in Chapter 12 on page 147. In the case of the Barn-Wall example the only major change was the increase in clerical workers. Take a moment to summarize your findings about changes in social class composition when the hospital closed in Crestview and most of the medical profession was forced to leave the community.

Interpret the results of your analysis for SIA #16

_____

_____

_____

_____

_____

_____

**Table 9.4 Changes in Occupational Categories (New Social Classes)
- Percent of Total Area Jobs (data from Table 8.9)**

Occupational Category (Barn-Wall example)	<u>Your Community</u>			<u>Barn-Wall Store</u>		
	Percent Employed	Percent Employed w/wo Project	Percent Change (+/-)	Percent Employed	Percent Employed w/wo Project	Percent Change (+/-)
_____ (Farm Operators)	____	____	____	29	27	-2
_____ (Clerical/ Sales)	____	____	____	15	19	+4
_____ (Craftsman/ Foreman)	____	____	____	7	6	-1
_____	____	____	____	____	____	____
_____	____	____	____	____	____	____
_____	____	____	____	____	____	____

REMINDER: *Before you go to the next social impact assessment variable it is important to remember that your goal is to understand what will likely happen in your community as a result of the <u>proposed action</u> so community leaders and project proponents can work together to maximize the benefits and minimize the costs. The presence of interested and dedicated newcomers could do much to revitalize a community that has lost a professional or managerial class.* ***As an assessor, you do not make judgments or value statements about the <u>proposed action</u>!***

SIA 18. Assessing Change in the Commercial/Industrial Focus of the Community

Definition: This variable refers to the change in the traditional commercial/industrial (private) or public sector focus of the community as a result of the proposed action. A change in focus would take place once a project is in operation or after the abandonment (closing) phase.

Instructions: **Why do we need to understand shifts in the commercial/industrial focus of a community?** If the project under consideration is large in terms of number of employees and income generated, and/or the community area is of low economic diversification, a change in the *focus* of the community may take place. For example, if the area under study is known as a retirement, college, farming, ranching or other type of community, residents might be concerned that the proposed action will change the traditional character. If it does, the change may alter existing social relationships and affect residents' lifestyles and their perceptions of their community. It may also affect the image outsiders have of the area, and, in turn, decisions of families or public and private sector activities to locate in the community. In the State of Illinois, many communities have competed to host new maximum security prisons. While the job and incentive benefits may be great, the definition of the community will likely change when a prison and those in it become the "new neighbor". When accepting a prison facility, community leaders should consider personal and family security concerns (even though they may be only perceptual) as well as how such a perception of their community would influence the opportunities for attracting other businesses to the area.

> "Changing residents' perceptions of their community does not happen overnight. One's identity is tied up in jobs...particularly if they are tied to community location."

Step 1. There are at least two methods of measuring this variable. Most states in the U.S. and Canadian provinces classify communities on the basis of population size and the type of retail trade. For example, in the State of Illinois the classifications are rural manufacturing, rural agriculture, rural diversified, down state metropolitan, and Chicago with suburbs. Table 9.5 provides space to write the classification description of the community you are assessing. Do you think this classification might change as a result of the proposed development? **Yes?** ☐ **No?** ☐

For example, Arvana, where **Acme Waste Management** is considering locating a waste disposal site, has a population of 4,500 and is classified as rural agriculture. If **Acme Waste** locates a facility in this community, it is likely that ancillary businesses may also locate here. As a result, it is possible that the classification of this community may change to rural diversified (or, worse yet, a garbage town) which may affect the image of that community, both for the residents and to outsiders.

Step 2. Determining the Nature of Community Identity.

A. Complete Table 9.5 for your development event. You may have already collected this information in Activity 6.2.

Table 9.5 Changes in Commercial/Industrial Focus

Community	Present Classification	Projected Classification
Arvana (Acme Waste Management)	Agriculture	Rural diversified
Your Community	_____	_____

B. A second measure involves an evaluation of residents' perceptions of their community, based on informal observations or available needs assessment studies. Examples of labels include a college town, a farm village or a retirement community. As part of the visioning process, many communities have outlined a path for their future. Based on this information you should be able to determine whether the proposed action would result in a change in that image. Enter your response in Table 9.6 based on either community observation or data from a community-wide visioning process.

Table 9.6 Changes in Commercial/Industrial Focus From Observation or Formal Studies

Community	Label from Needs Assessment Study	Projected Label after development
Arvana (Waste Management)	rural	garbage town
Butchart (Canadian Dream)	pastoral	destination resort
Forks, Washington	timber town	prison town
Your Community	_____	_____

Step 3.

Enter Significant Results. If you do not have access to data from a community assessment, or the proposed project will not change the focus of the impacted community, go on to SIA #19. However, if the perception of the community will change based on the <u>proposed action</u>, enter the information from Table 9.6 in Chapter 12, on page 148.

SIA 19. Assessing the Presence of Weekend Residents

Definition: The presence of weekend residents refers to the influx of weekend or short term visitors who do not have a permanent home in the community. This variable applies, for example, to the operation/maintenance stage of a large recreation facility such as the Lake Shelbyville Reservoir in Central Illinois (U.S.). Visitors from cruise ships would be another example.

Instructions: **Why is it important to understand the impacts of weekend residents?** One of the most important social impacts is the *weekend resident syndrome*. People come to an area to partake of a particular recreational, historical or cultural opportunity without living in the community. The attraction for outsiders visiting your community may have been created by development, such as casino gambling on tribal lands in the U.S., or by a policy change such as purchase of land for the Shawnee National Forest in Southern Illinois or a new reservoir. The weekend residents may use the new recreational or tourism opportunity, yet contribute very little to the host community. This SIA variable is intended to alert community leaders to the opportunities, which may result from the influx of large numbers of persons on a temporary basis. Communities cannot reap the benefits of recreational visitors unless they plan in advance to provide the needed services. The docking of cruise ships on a Caribbean Island means thousands of visitors pour into a community, but stay only a few hours.

> "Tourists are fine as long as we get them to spend their money (meaning in our community.)" Mayor of Cairns, Northern Queensland, Australia

The **Canadian Dream** residential development is one such example. This development will result in the construction of a public golf course, a large recreational lake, tennis courts, and other recreational facilities that will likely draw non-residents on weekends and holidays. Those weekend residents need services ranging from adequate accommodations and campsites to emergency medical service. The financial success of the proposed development will depend upon how well these needs are met. Put another way, how can the community attract and keep visitor expenditures? Another indicator of short term residents is the number of vacant housing units at the time of an off season census

Step 1. **Data to determine the number of weekend residents.**

The project proponent should provide estimates on the number of average weekend residents who might visit the facility. These estimates come from attendance records for similar facilities. If new or expanded tourism or recreational development is a component of the proposed project, enter the number of estimated visitors in Table 9.7.

Step 2. **Determine the amount of lodging and campsites available in the area.**

The number of rooms in hotels, motels, guest homes, bed and breakfasts, hostels, and campsites can be obtained from the Chamber of Commerce or Tourism and Visitors Offices. This number should be entered into Table 9.7

Table 9.7 Changes in Weekend Residents and Short Term Visitors

	Your Community	Canadian Dream
Current Population	_____	4,700
# Weekend Residents	_____	800
Percent Change	_____	+17%
# of Rooms/Campsite Available**	_____	25
# of Weekend Residents Housed in Area	_____	100
# Weekend Residents who need Accommodation	_____	700

**Refers to the number available within the primary and secondary zones of influence.

Step 2.   **Enter Significant Results.** If the percentage of visitors is over 10% of the persons living in the community, enter the information from Table 9.7 in Chapter 12 on page 148. If the number of weekend residents exceeds available accommodation by 50, enter this in Table 9.7 in Chapter 12 on page 148. Much of the benefit of recreational development will be lost if weekend residents must leave the area for accommodation or the purchase of food and recreational supplies. Communities that attract cruise ships must build expensive docking facilities and short term recreation and shopping opportunities. How do these communities attract and keep visitor expenditures when the cruise ship traffic is seasonal and participants are only in town for a few hours? Seasonal employees to support the cruise ships traffic will require expanded infrastructure facilities.

Evaluate the results of your analysis for SIA #19

_____

_____

_____

_____

_____

Summary of Chapter 9

Each of the SIA variables outlined in this chapter will help you understand the type of tensions which may occur as new developments produce community change. Using the illustrations as a guideline complete Table 9.8 using the information you have obtained for the five *communities in transition* SIA variables.

Table 9.8 Communities in Transition

Variables Describing Communities in Transition	Your Community	Acme Waste Mgt. (Siting)	Barn-Wall (Business)	Crestview Hospital (Closing)	Canadian Dream (Housing)
15. Presence of an outside agency...	_____	Yes	Yes	No	Yes
16. Level of inter-organizational cooperation	_____	Low	OK	Low	Low
17. Introduction of new social classes...	_____	No	No	Yes	Yes
18. Change in the commercial/Industrial focus of the community...	_____	Yes	No	Yes	Yes
19. Presence of weekend residents (recreational)...	_____	No	No	No	Yes

On to Chapter 10

Chapter 10. Individual and Family Level Impacts

How will the project or policy change alter the lives of individuals and families in your assessment community?

The objective of this chapter is to measure the impacts of the proposed action on family structure and the day-to-day activity of individuals. We are also concerned as to how the proposed action might influence individual well-being to include perceptions of health and safety, disruption in established social networks and daily living and movement patterns. In addition, change in leisure opportunities might result from the proposed action. Different cultural and religious practices in the area might influence the benefits of proponent proposals.

Many of the impacts discussed in this chapter would normally occur during the planning and construction phases, but may occur at all stages of the environmental and social impact assessment process.

➡

SIA 20. Assessing the Disruption in Daily Living and Movement Patterns

Definition: SIA #20 refers to changes or disruptions in the routine of daily living and work activities caused by alteration to the visual environment, noise and odor levels, transportation routes or the amount of vehicular traffic resulting from the <u>proposed action</u>.

Instructions: **What is important about disruption in daily living and movement patterns?** Construction and operation may cause adverse environmental change leading residents in the vicinity to alter their movement patterns and social habits to minimize exposure to project related activity. Such adverse impacts include for example, increased traffic congestion, noise, odor, air or water pollution and unsightly facilities. The latter is important because it can affect residents' perceptions of their community (which in turn may affect how willing they are to continue to invest time and tax money) and how likely they are to move elsewhere. Experiments have shown that noise levels affect performance, feelings of well-being, and perceptions of the quality of the environment where people live. Research has also shown that excessive odor and poor air quality impact daily living. In addition, there are definite health and safety risks associated with excessive noise and persistent traffic congestion. Visual impacts may be more subjective, but research has shown that a more pleasing visual environment has definite effects on one's sense of well-being. Most of the disruptions listed in Table 10.1 are temporary in nature and a public information program likely will minimize most problems. Generally speaking, citizens are willing to alter movement patterns if they know about the changes **in advance**.

> Oftentimes, simply telling people in advance what will happen is enough to minimize controversy…

Step 1.   **Determining the Significance of Project Related Disruptions.**

A.   As a result of the proposed project, will any of the situations or disruptions listed in Table 10.1 take place during the construction, operation/maintenance or decommissioning phase? Yes ☐   No ☐; If No, go to SIA #21 in the next section.

If Yes, data to complete Table 10.1 may be obtained from the project proponent or from community observation.

B.   Describe in some detail the disruptions in the community under assessment (the map you used in a previous section will help here).

_____

_____

_____

Table 10.1 Disruption in Daily Living/Movement Patterns

Type of Disruption	Your Community		Acme Waste Mgt.	
	Yes	No	Yes	No
Increased noise	___	___	X	
Foul or unusual odors	___	___		X
Increased air pollution	___	___	X	
Dust and commotion	___	___	X	
Increased vehicular traffic	___	___	X	
Visual Alteration	___	___	X	
Polluted waters	___	___		?
Closed roads and bridges	___	___	X	
Disruption of utilities	___	___	X	
Other temporary closures	___	___	?	
Nuclear contamination	___	___		X
Other _____	___	___	___	___

Step 2. **Enter Significant Results.**

Enter the disruptions shown in Table 10.1 on page 149 in Chapter 12.

Evaluate the results of your analysis for SIA # 20

_____

_____

_____

_____

_____

SIA 21. Assessing the Dissimilarity in Religious and Cultural Practices

Definition: This social impact variable refers to the introduction into your community of a new group of persons with religious and cultural values, beliefs and practices dissimilar to those of the present population. This variable is most observable during planning construction and the operation/maintenance phase.

Instructions: **Why should we be aware of differences in religious and cultural practices?** If persons with different religious and cultural backgrounds move into the community, significant social changes may occur. For example, your community may be dominated by a single religious group which has a strong influence on local lifestyles and political decisions. If the new population does not share a religious background with present residents, conflict is likely. In 1985, the Kedungombo Dam and Irrigation Project in Central Java (Indonesia) was funded by the World Bank. In the process of resettlement of 5,390 households in 38 villages, the sacred remains of ancestors were either flooded or removed. The Moslem population in this area would pray next to the remains of their ancestors. Also in Indonesia, the government started a lottery, which included the Moslem population of Java, without realizing that the lottery is considered gambling and prohibited by religious custom. Conflict over religious beliefs and cultural practices is becoming more frequent in many parts of the world. Although easily dismissed, you will be well served to look for possible conflicts between cultural practices and the proposed action.

> North Sea oil drilling has brought many changes to Scotland...some humorous. A local schoolmaster was shocked one September morning to find 33 new French-speaking (only) students at the school door.

In our example, the community in which **Acme Waste Management** is building a waste disposal facility is a rural community composed exclusively of Caucasians. Construction workers will most likely be hired from a larger metropolitan area because of the specialized skills needed to construct such a facility. As a result, it is possible that the firm will employ non-Caucasian workers with different religious/cultural practices than those of the community residents. You must research and show this possibility in Table 10.2.

Step 1. **Questions to analyze for your project setting.**

A. Would major religious or cultural groups in the community be seen by outsiders as different? Yes ❑ No ❑

B. Is it likely that a distinct religious and/or cultural group will be brought into the community during the construction and/or operation phase of the proposed project? Yes ❑ No ❑.

Step 2. If the answer is **Yes** to either question, complete Table 10.2 and describe the nature of the difference in Step 3 and in Chapter 12 on page 150.

Table 10.2
Differences in Religious & Cultural Practices

	Your Community		Acme Waste Management	
	Present	Projected	Present	Projected
Differences in Religious and Cultural practices	_____	_____	No	No

Step 3. Describe possible differences in cultural and religious practices.

_____

_____

_____

SIA 22. Assessing the Alteration in Family Structure

Definition: Alteration in family structure involves an increase or decrease in one or more of the family status categories (e.g., married, never married, female head of household, with/without children) as a result of the proposed action or other change in the community. These changes may be temporary during construction phase or long term if it occurs during the operation and maintenance phase.

Instructions: **Why is alteration in family structure important?** There are at least three ways to examine the alteration in family structure variable. The *first* is to look for differences between the family structure of the community and that of the persons who will arrive as a result of the proposed action. *One example* is the introduction of a construction work force of single males into a remote, family-centered community. A *second* would be to examine how employment changes might affect the marital structure of the present community. Will new employment opportunities go to females, as in the case of hotel and motel development or the building of a "big-box store", leaving males to assume traditional female household roles? A *third* approach would be to examine communities which are experiencing out-migration brought on by employment opportunities in other locations. In South Africa, for example, black males routinely migrate long distances for construction jobs or to work in the *"mines"* and leave females in the villages to care for the children and livestock.

As noted, the construction phase will bring a large number of young males into the community. Many will be single and those who are married may not be accompanied by their families. The *single* male, construction worker phenomena is more likely if the project is lengthy, if temporary or rental housing is in short supply, and if both labor and materials must be brought in from long distances. If the newcomers are predominantly young and male, their acceptance and integration may be difficult if the community is isolated with a focus on religious and family traditions. Research on social impacts has shown that drunkenness, increased crime, general rowdiness, harassment and even rape may accompany the population influx of unaccompanied males. Their behaviors are often a violation of traditional community norms and informal social controls seldom work for these new arrivals. The construction of the **Acme Waste** facility was a lengthy operation requiring both labor and materials to be brought from distant trade centers. These issues was further inflamed by the behavior of construction workers who, among other activities, scattered beer cans each afternoon between the construction site and a temporary housing facility in Arvana.

A change in employment opportunities for your community may lead to significant change in the family structure. On the benefit side, new development may keep families in the area that might otherwise leave. Dependency ratios tend to be higher in rural than in urban areas due to the large number of children and older people. Younger persons tend to stay in the community if new job opportunities provide a living wage (see SIA#11).

Step 1.   **Data for Measuring Change in Family Structure.**

A. Calculate the dependency ratio for your community.

The **dependency ratio** is total number of employed persons in the community divided by the population over 16 years of age.
Write that ratio here (.....................) and if the ratio for the impact community is less than .62 enter on page 151 of Chapter 12.

Dependency ratios of less than .62 indicate fewer wage earners to support the population. Higher dependency ratios generally indicate more families above the poverty line. **http://www.bls.gov/**

B. Using data from the recent census and information obtained from the project proponent complete Table 10.3.

Step 2.   **Enter Significant Results.**
If the differences in marital status categories between present residents and newcomers is greater than 10 percent significant social impacts could be present. Enter this information in Chapter 12 on page 150.

Table 10.3 Changes in Family Structure and Composition

Population over 18 years	Your Community			Acme Waste		
	Presently	Newcomers	+/-	Presently	Newcomers	+/-
% Married	____	____	___	65	50	-15
% Never Married	____	____	___	10	40	+30
% Divorced	____	____	___	5	10	+5
% Widow(er)	____	____	___	20	0	-20

SIA 23. Assessing the Disruption of Social Networks

Definition: SIA #23 refers to the termination or disruption of normal community social interaction patterns (including friendship and kin relations) by project activity. This effect may be temporary, as in the blocking of roads during construction or permanent, if natural or construed barriers block physical access. This variable also includes persons living next to but who were not required to move due to highway, reservoir or other construction settings.

Instructions: **Why should we be concerned with possible disruptions in family and neighborhood social networks?** The usual flow of social interaction and communication within the community may be disrupted by project related activity. An example would be the construction of physical barriers such as roads, reservoirs, railroads, power lines, and commercial centers which block or alter existing vehicular or pedestrian routes.

> Social networks are disrupted when highways are built. Those not relocated had the most difficulty in re-establishing support networks due to physical barriers.

A corresponding disruption in social networks will affect some individuals more than others. For example, persons with low incomes may be unable to afford the increased time and expense to continue former social relationships. The elderly and physically handicapped may be cut off from family support networks. The disruption of social networks will always occur in the case of significant population relocation, particularly if due to reservoirs and canals, highway or rail construction, pipelines, or other types of linear development. In addition access to churches, schools, health care and other essential services may be disrupted.

In the case of the **Canadian Dream** residential development, the construction of a 300-hectare lake and an additional 900 hectares of residential units will result in blocking roads that had served to connect rural neighbors to each other and to the town for shopping, medical visits and socializing. It is important that these blockages be analyzed to determine how many people or households are affected. If more than 15 households will be changed from normal travel routes, it is likely that this social impact will be significant.

Step 1.   **Procedures to Analyze Disruptions in Social Networks.**

A.   If the proposed project includes the construction of linear developments which will alter, split, disrupt or in any way sever present neighborhoods, communities, settlements or family and cultural groups, complete Table 10.4 using proponent information, maps of the area and census data on the population composition of community residents.

B.   You must also determine if low income or minority persons are disproportionately affected by the proposed project.

Table 10.4 Disruptions in Social Networks

	Your Community	**Canadian Dream**
Number of Households Affected	_____	40
% Of Affected Households Low Income/Poverty level?	_____	15
% Of Affected Households Racial, Ethnic and/or Native?	_____	None
% Of Affected Households With Persons Over 65?	_____	20
% Of Affected Households Of Distinct Religious or Cultural Groups?	_____	None

Step 2.   **Enter Significant Results.**

If the percent of households affected is greater than 15 percent, enter this information in Chapter 12 on page 151.

Evaluate the results of your analysis for SIA # 23

_____

_____

SIA 24. Assessing Perceptions of Public Health and Safety

Definition: This SIA variable refers to a perception, attitude or belief on the part of community residents that their physical health and safety as well as their mental well-being will be affected by the proposed action. Perceptions, attitudes, and beliefs about health and safety must be treated as real with real consequences and they may occur at any stage.

Instruction: **Why are perceptions of public health and safety important?** One of the major social impacts of a proposed project, be it the siting of a hazardous waste facility, the location of a new landfill, or hog confinement buildings, is the anxiety and fears it may produce amongst local residents. While the public's assessment of risk is perceptual in nature, their fears should not be dismissed as irrational and therefore unimportant. If there is a widespread belief that the project will endanger the mental and physical health of present and future generations, community acceptance of and support for the project will be less than enthusiastic. Citizens will weigh the potential benefits of the project to the community against their perceptions of associated risk.

Step 1. **Where do you find information to measure perception and risk?** Use guidelines from Chapter 6 and some of the same sources outlined for SIA #'s 6 & 7 in Chapter 8 which include newspaper articles, the transcripts of hearings, workshops, and advisory councils, or similar settings where the public was invited to comment. Solicit informal views from a representative cross-section of the community, since perceptions of risk and personal well-being will vary widely, depending upon proximity to the proposed project. If citizens were contacted as part of the planning process, during scoping, or at the initiative of stakeholders, by all means use this information.

> The public health and safety portion of an SIA must be included in the larger environmental impact assessment (EIA).

The citizens of Arvana have reservations about the waste disposal facility proposed by **Acme Waste Management**. At the public hearing, concerns were raised about health (cancer or lung diseases), safety due to increased traffic and contamination of ground water and residential drinking wells. People wondered about the operational phase of the project when waste is brought into the community from other areas. But they also worry about what will happen when the facility is closed and who will be responsible for monitoring long term environmental and health effects.

Step 2. **Analyzing Perceptions of Public Health and Safety.**

Complete the questions listed in Table 10.5 using public participation sources (Chapter 6) such as surveys, testimonial, bibliographic, public hearings, letters, newspapers or other written and observational data from the study area.

**Table 10.5 Perceptions of Public Health and Safety
(Based on evidence from public participation sources and community observations)**

Perceptions	Your Community No	Yes	Arvana (Waste Mgt) No	Yes
Air pollution and dust	___	___		X
Noise levels	___	___	X	
Nuclear fallout	___	___	X	
Vehicular accidents	___	___		X
Odors and smells	___	___		X
Environmental degradation	___	___		X
Surface water pollution	___	___		X
Groundwater contamination	___	___		X
Drinking contaminated water	___	___		X
Others_____	___	___	___	___
_____	___	___	___	___

Step 3.   **Enter Significant Results.**

If any categories of persons in the study community have expressed fears of personal health and safety as a result of the proposed project, enter beside the appropriate category and in Table 10.5 and on page 152 in Chapter 12. *Perceptions of public health and safety* is a social impact assessment variable which is required in the larger environmental and social impact assessment.

Evaluate the results of your analysis for SIA # 24

_____

_____

_____

_____

SIA 25. Assessing Change in Leisure Opportunities

Definition: SIA #25 refers to an increase or decrease in leisure/recreational opportunities within the community due to a change in the management of a natural resource area, the development of a new recreation facility or a facility with a major recreation component.

Instructions: **Why should we analyze changes in leisure opportunities?** The number and type of leisure and recreational opportunities available in a community has an important influence on residents' satisfaction. Recreational (e.g., commercial and municipal) and natural resource based recreation (e.g., water related and water enhanced outdoor recreation) may add to, or change the nature of available leisure opportunities. Not only will residents be affected, but outsider perceptions of the community may change and thereby influence the number of people and businesses that relocate into or out of the area in the future.

> "…now that the (Eagle Creek) resort is operating, my wife and I have a decent restaurant when we celebrate our anniversary."
>
> Mayor of Shelbyville, Illinois

Most rural communities and counties lack year round recreation facilities for all age categories. Data from needs assessment studies show that people simply want more residential recreational opportunity. As we found in an earlier chapter, the development of a major recreation area (such as the Lake Shelbyville reservoir in Central Illinois, U.S.) produced a large influx of seasonal *weekend* or *vacation* residents. Often overlooked during project planning--is that present community residents will be the biggest users of a new recreation facility (60 percent of the users of Lake Shelbyville come from the two counties where the reservoir is located). While the Eagle Creek Resort in Shelby County was built to bring convention and tourist trade to the area, it also provided a quality restaurant and resort facilities for local residents.

📖 *Concepts,* Chapter 14.

While the construction of the 300-hectare lake, golf courses, tennis courts and other recreational facilities at the **Canadian Dream** development is designed to attract permanent and seasonal residents to the project, it will also provide recreational opportunities for residents of Butchart and neighboring municipalities. If however, these new recreational facilities are available only to paid members or residents of the development, the benefits to local residents will be diminished. As a condition of project approval, the municipality should insist that the recreation facilities be available to community residents.

Step 1. **Obtaining data to measure recreational opportunity in the project area.**

A. Is a recreation facility development (or closure) a part of the proposed project? Yes ☐ No ☐. If No, go to Table 10.7.

B. If the proposed development will provide new recreational and leisure facilities and opportunities that are not now available within your community, complete Table 10.6 from information obtained from the project proponent and the local municipality.

Table 10.6 Changes in Leisure Opportunities for Community Residents

Leisure Opportunity	Present Situation	Without Development	Present Situation	Canadian Dream
Swim pools (.25)	_____	_____	No	Yes
Boating areas	_____	_____	No	Yes
Camping sites	_____	_____	No	No
Playgrounds (1.25)	_____	_____	No	Yes
Picnic tables (4.0)	_____	_____	No	Yes
Fishing ponds	_____	_____	Yes	Yes
Golf courses (.13)	_____	_____	No	Yes
Tennis courts (.50)	_____	_____	No	Yes
Nature center	_____	_____	No	Yes
Youth center	_____	_____	No	No
Senior center	_____	_____	No	No
Miles(km) of Walking Path (.50)	_____	_____	None	10km
Miles (km) of Bike Paths (.71)	_____	_____	None	12km
Other facilities	_____	_____	_____	_____

Step 2. **Enter Significant Results.** If the proposed development will provide leisure and recreational opportunity for local residents, enter those opportunities in Chapter 12 on page 153. ✆ **www.nrpa.org/** The National Recreation and Park Association has a list of recreation facility levels of service for many types of recreation activities-based on 1,000 population. The numbers shown in (parentheses) table 10.6 are U.S. only standards from the NRPA "yellow book*" Recreation, Park, and Open Space Standards and Guidelines* (1983) .

Summary of Chapter 10

Table 10.7 shows which individual and family level impacts are likely to occur for each of the examples used in this book. Using the illustrations as guidelines, complete the table using the information you have obtained for the six individual and family level social impact assessment variables.

Your SIA Project _____

Table 10.7 Summary of Individual and Family Level Impacts

Individual and Family Level Impact Variables	Your Community	Waste Mgt. (Siting)	Barn-Wall (Business)	Crestview Hospital (Closing)	Canadian Dream (Housing)
20. Disruption in daily living and movement patterns	_____	Yes	Possible	No	Yes
21. Dissimilarity in religious practices	_____	Possible	No	No	Possible
22. Alteration in family structure	_____	No	Possible	Likely	Yes
23. Disruption in social networks	_____	Possible	No	Possible	Likely
24. Perceptions of public health and safety	_____	Yes	No	Yes	Yes
25. Change in leisure opportunities	_____	No	No	No	Yes

Go to Chapter 11

Chapter 11. Community Infrastructure Needs

How will the proposed project alter the infrastructure and service needs of the impacted community?

Community infrastructure needs include everything from a new sewage system to roads, hospitals, and police—in short, everything that happens to the physical and organizational structure of the area that supports human populations. Also included under this category are the SIA variables "land acquisition and disposal" and the possible presence of "cultural, historical, sacred and archeological sites."

The objectives of this chapter are to determine how the proposed project or policy change may alter:

1. Your community's infrastructure.

2. The service needs of your community.

3. Land ownership patterns and property values.

4. Cultural, historical, sacred and archeological sites.

SIA 26. Assessing Change in Community Infrastructure

By community infrastructure we mean an increase or decrease in the requirements for and supply of basic infrastructure facilities and services within the community as a result of the proposed action.

Instructions: **Why is community infrastructure important?** Development alters the requirements (need) for private sector and community services and facilities. Community infrastructure includes roads, sewers, health care and hospital facilities, medical personnel, health care inspectors, private and public sector housing, police and fire protection, bridges, water, electricity and other utilities, recreational facilities, education and library facilities, and more. In the U.S., most of the community infrastructure is paid for by local property taxes and fees, with occasional state and federal help. There are actually two components of community infrastructure: the physical infrastructure and the municipal/city and county and private sector support services.

> Having a well-maintained and up-to-date community infrastructure is the key toward realizing project benefits and revitalizing depressed communities.

Developing a new project or closing an old one may lead to shortages or excesses of infrastructure and services. Good community infrastructure enhances the benefits of new projects and ensures that these benefits stay in the community. For example, the population influx that accompanies construction may result in expanded or new facilities or, alternatively if closed, to reduced community service levels. Communities should invest in new facilities for long term needs, not short run development. Rental housing is often in short supply in rural and remote communities. Therefore, available housing should be inventoried, since construction and service related projects often lead to demand for existing housing and thus increases building costs and higher rents.

In the long term, the revenues local governments derive from new projects through an increased tax base may support an expanded infrastructure. However, in the short term, local government may need money for expanded services before tax revenues from the project become available.

Community infrastructure variables are included in the social impact assessment portion of a required environmental impact statement since the cost and quality of public services has an influence on residents' sense of well-being and satisfaction with their community. These *changes in community infrastructure needs* as well as the question of who pays are frequently overlooked in the rush to bring development and occupational opportunities to economically depressed areas. However, addressing community infrastructure needs is a key component in the step toward realizing project benefits and the revitalization of depressed communities.

Step 1.   **Procedures to analyze community infrastructure needs.**

Finding data to analyze this SIA variable will require locating standards (or thresholds) for the delivery of community services as well as a lot of *detective work* in your community. A common reaction is "*...we have been losing people for years, so why do we need to look at expanding community services?*" Boarded up stores, abandoned houses and dilapidated schools are indicators of dying communities. However, the delivery of most community services requires human capital in the form of a competent community/municipal administrative structure.

Most services are expressed in terms of the amount needed per 1,000 persons; called either standards, levels of service or thresholds.

A.   Write the total population of your community (or other geographical unit as appropriate) in this space divided by 1,000 = _____ .

This factor is the population multiplier for your study area. Each of the components of community infrastructure should be multiplied by the community infrastructure needs factor.

B.   Enter the required number for each infrastructure item in Table 11.1.

C.   Next answer the following questions which are also included in the environmental impact assessment (EIA).

    1) Is the municipal sewer system in compliance with state, provincial and federal standards? Yes☐   No☐.

    2) Number of additional housing or commercial units allowed until the sewer system reaches capacity: _____ (#)

    3) Do the municipal water and/or rural water district meet state, provincial or federal safe drinking standards? Yes ☐   No ☐

    4) Is any state, provincial or federally designated "wetlands" in the project area? Yes ☐   No ☐

Step 2.   **Enter Significant Results**

If you have infrastructure and public and private sector service differences greater than **-10** or **+10**, or you answered **No** to 1) and 3) in C above you either have excessive infrastructure to maintain, or excess capacity which could be helpful if the community or municipality anticipates expansion. Enter all significant results in Chapter 12 on page 154.

☞ Possible web sites include: www.icma.org/ , www.nic.org/ www.naco.org/ , www.nrpa.org/ Service and facility standards vary in different parts of the world, so check locally.

Table 11.1 Changes in Community Infrastructure

Community Infrastructure	Your Community			Barn-Wall Store[a]		
	Present Situation	Number With Project	Variance (+ or -)	Present Situation	Darnell Number Required	Variance (+ or -)
Police/Sheriffs (2.1)				3.5	7.8	-4.3
Patrol Cars (1.1)				2	4.1	-2.3
Firefighters (1.5)				4.5	5.5	-1.0
Medic units (.25)				0	0.9	-0.9
Hospital Beds (3.3)				10	12.2	-2.2
Physicians (.9)				1	3.3	-2.3
Dentists (.8)				1	3.0	-2.0
Nurses (.7)				2	2.6	-0.6
Certified Teachers (4.8)				15	17.7	-2.7
Adult/juvenile detention (3.6)*				9	13.3	-4.3
Libraries (700 sq. ft)*				1	1.0	0.0
Acres of parkland (10.0)				12	37.0	-25.0
Acres of open space (12.5)				25	46.2	-21.2
Linear trails in miles (1.0)				3	3.7	-0.7
Other _____ (___)						
Standards per 1,000 persons.		Totals =			Totals =	-69.5

[a] Note: the population of Darnell is 3,700 - therefore, the multiplier is 3.7. *Detention facilities in beds and library space expressed in square feet.

NOTES ON YOUR COMMUNITY'S INFRASTRUCTURE NEEDS

_____

_____

_____

_____

_____

_____

_____

_____

_____

_____

_____

_____

_____

_____

_____

_____

_____

SIA 27. Assessing Land Acquisition and Disposal

SIA #27 refers to the total number of acres (hectares) of land that will change from present use classification or ownership as a result of the proposed action. This variable may involve land transfers from one governmental jurisdictional unit to another or from private sector to public ownership and in some cases public to private.

Instructions: **Why should we analyze changes in land ownership?**

...to benefit from development, we must make sure funds or fees are available to pay for community infrastructure needs in advance.

Land acquisition or disposal resulting from the project could represent more than a financial loss or gain to the community. If the project is controversial, residents may object to land acquisition. If private land is to become public, the change may represent a loss to the local tax base, in that public property is not always subject to local, state or provincial taxes. Such a tax loss may mean public services and facilities in the area are either reduced or the remaining taxpayers will be asked to pay more. As an incentive to locate in the community, new businesses and industry are often "forgiven" a portion of the property or goods and services taxes they would normally pay. While this is useful in attracting new business and industry, it does shift a greater proportion of the community tax burden to present property owners, existing businesses and private citizens.

Governmental assistance may be necessary if increased demands on community infrastructure result from project-induced population growth. If the project is to be sited on publicly owned land, a change in federal or state land management policy may affect local residents. For example, wilderness designation of federal forests or crown lands will alter the type of access to the land and restrict such uses as logging, grazing, mining and motorized vehicles. These commercial and recreational activities may have been important to the local economy. Where the project entails change in land tenure (e.g., issuing permits allowing private development on public land) rapid commercial development may occur in areas lacking adequate zoning controls (SIA #9). Such development could, in turn, lead to significant biophysical impacts on nearby private land, local economies and the capacity of local government to provide services.

Local governments are strapped for cash and often approve projects that increase property values, provide sales tax revenues or "impact fees." Impact fees are used for storm and sanitary sewers, parks and recreation development, water treatment, roads and streets and sometimes schools.

The proposed construction of the **Acme Waste Landfill**, for example, will require the acquisition of 450 acres of farm land. The land will change ownership, but will remain in the private sector; however because of higher valuation, the landfill will increase local property tax revenues.

Step 1. **Analyzing Changes in Land Use.**

A. Complete Table 11.2 for the proposed development utilizing information from the project proponent and the county, municipal, township or village tax assessment office. For an example of the components included in a local/municipal tax assessment go to **www.whatcomcounty.us/** and look under property recording and taxes.

B. Use shadow pricing for determining new property valuations. If more than one property use is involved, the estimates must be completed on a parcel-by-parcel basis.

C. Will the project require zoning changes? Yes ☐   No ☐

Table 11.2 Land Acquisition and Disposal

	Your Community	Arvana
Number of Acres (Hectare) in Project	_____	450
Private or Public (Without Project)	_____	Private
Private or Public (With Project)	_____	Private
Assessed Property Value for Taxes (Without Project)	_____	$180,000
Assessed Property Value for Taxes after Change (With Project)	_____	$ 5 ,000,000
Change in Assessed Value	_____	+$4,820.000 (+2,678%)
Sales Tax Revenue Change	_____	Not Available

Step 2. **Enter Significant Results.**

A. If the proposed project involves the transfer of property from private to public ownership or if the tax assessment is projected to increase or decrease by more than 10%, or if a zoning change is required, enter the information on page 156 in Chapter 12.

Summarize the results of your analysis for SIA #27

_____

_____

SIA 28. Assessing Effects on Known Cultural, Historical, Sacred and Archaeological Resources

This variable refers to possible destruction, diminution or alteration of one or more of the known cultural/historical/sacred or archeological resources within the assessment area as a result of the proposed action.

Instructions: **Why is it important?**

Most of the sacred and spiritual sites are from Aboriginal, First Nation or other indigenous populations. Some have been mapped by archeologists and anthropologists in their attempts to reconstruct the history of the culture and the organization of present and past societies. A sacred site refers to an area of religious or cultural significance to present day indigenous and Aboriginal populations. Some are known, while others may intentionally be secret. Once a sacred site is known to outsiders it may lose its sacred and cultural significance. In addition, some Tribes, Aboriginal people and First Nations may have subsistence hunting, fishing, and gathering rights in the area.

> Tribal leaders warned the Mayor of Denver that the proposed airport would never work right because it was to be built on a sacred Ute Indian site! They were right—it never worked

In the U.S., Canada, and former colonies the term **folk culture** refers to the artifacts and structures of the European settlers. Examples would be old buildings, churches, monuments, historic sites and even entire towns. Community members are often proud of their cultural, historical and archeological resources. Thus, their destruction or alteration could not only mean the loss of valuable historic sites but may also lead to an increase in public opposition to the project and may delay approval. Losing such resources may be perceived by residents as detracting from the community and lead to local opposition.

Step 1. **Sources of Data.**

A. Data to assess this variable come from the state or provincial historic preservation officer, the tribal or Aboriginal preservation office and the register of historic places. Some countries have antiquities acts and legislation to protect folk culture. Antiquity legislation prohibits the unauthorized excavation, removal or damage of "archeological resources". In the U.S., an example of folk culture would be the protection of Colonial Williamsburg, in the present State of Virginia.

B. Will the proposed project destroy, alter or in any way change a known cultural, historical, sacred or archeological site? As mentioned above, information for this assessment is available from First Nations, Tribes, state, municipal or provincial historical societies or the office of the official state or provincial archeologist. Yes ☐   No ☐

If **No**, go to Table 11.4. If **Yes**, complete Table 11.3.

Table 11.3 Effects on Cultural, Historical, Sacred and Archeological Resources

Resource	Your Community		Arvana	
	Yes	No	Yes	No
Registered Historical Site (e.g. National Historic Register)	____	____		X
Certified Archeological/Antiquity Sites	____	____		X
Sacred or Spiritual Places	____	____		X
Cemeteries/Graves	____	____		X
State/Municipal/Local Parks	____	____		X
Proposed Historical Site Listing	____	____		X
Other_____	____	____		

Step 2.   **Enter Significant Results.**

If you checked **Yes** to any of the resource settings listed in Table 11.3, enter the information on page 156 in Chapter 12.

Describe the details of your analysis for SIA #28

_____

_____

_____

_____

_____

_____

_____

_____

Summary of Chapter 11.

Table 11.4 shows which community infrastructure impacts are likely to occur for each example used in this book. Complete the table using the information you have obtained for the three community infrastructure SIA variables.

Your Assessment Project: _____

Table 11.4 Summary of Community Infrastructure Impacts

Community Infrastructure Need Variables	Your Community	ACME Waste Mgmt. (Siting)	Barn-Wall (Business)	Crestview Hospital (Closing)	Canadian Dream (Housing)
	Enter Yes or No				
26. Change in community infrastructure.	_____	Yes	Yes	Yes	Yes
27. Land acquisition and disposal.	_____	Yes	Yes	No	Yes
28. Effects on known cultural, historical, sacred & archaeological resources.	_____	Possible	No	No	Possible

You have now completed gathering information on the social impacts of the proposed project or development for the community under assessment.

Congratulations! ☺ *You may now proceed to Chapter 12 where you will begin to put it all together.*

Chapter 12. Putting It All Together!

The goal of this chapter is to provide an overview of the important social impacts you must address as you assess the consequences of any proposed development or policy change.

Specific objectives for Chapter 12 are:

1. To evaluate the significance for each of the social impact assessment variables you transferred from Chapters 7-11.

2. To write a short analytical statement about each significant change.

3. To select the 10 to 15 most significant social impacts (changes) that will occur in the study community which will be dealt with by you the SIA practitioner, the social assessor, community leaders and the project proponent during mitigation (if the proposed action is approved).

4. To rank the list of social impact assessment variables. Your ranking will be used in Chapter 13 on mitigation, enhancement and monitoring.

Instructions: At this point in your SIA, you have transferred data about the proposed action for those SIA variables that might apply to your assessment. The next step is to test for significance and do a written interpretation of what your analysis means. The first step is to test for significance. I provide some hints on how to test for significance. Some may actually require statistical analysis, while others use only the presence or absence of the emperical change. You will get the idea after you have worked through a few of the tables.

Remember: **Unless impact setting you are assessing is really big, not all the SIA variables will apply!**

➡

SIA 1. Assessing Population Change from Table 7.1, page 63.

	Your Community's Population		Crestview Hospital	
	Before	After	Before	After
			9,400	8720
Difference (+ or -)		_____	-680	
%Change		_____	-7%	
Density (+ or -)		_____	-226/per sq. mi	

Analysis: _____

_____

Test for significance: Look for both percent and number change greater than 5% or a change of 500 persons.

SIA 2. Assessing influx or outflux of temporary workers from Table 7.2, page 65.

	Your Community	**Barn-Wall Development**
Percent and Number of Workers Hired from Outside the Community per Month.	_____	90% (50)
Length of Construction Period	_____	11 months

Analysis:_____

_____

_____

_____

_____

Test for significance: If the number of workers from outside the area is greater than 50 or 50% and the project is over 12 months.

SIA 3. *Assessing presence of seasonal (leisure) residents from Table 7.3, page 67.*

	Your Community	**Canadian Dream Development**
Current population	_____	4,700
Seasonal residents	_____	3,325
Percent of seasonal residents to current population	_____	70%

Analysis: _____

_____

_____

_____

Test for significance: If the percent of seasonal residents is greater than 15% of the resident population.

SIA 4. *Assessing the relocation of individuals and families from Table 7.4, page 69.*

	Your Community	**Acme Waste Site**
Persons Relocated	_____	65
Elderly, Poor as number and percent of persons relocated	_____	26 (40%)
Time Lapse till Move	_____	22 months

Analysis: _____

_____

_____

_____

Test for significance: If more than 50 persons (not households) are to be relocated and/or more than 25% are either poor and/or elderly. Also, if the time from notification of relocation until the actual move is greater than 18 months.

SIA 5. *Assessing the dissimilarity in age, gender, racial or ethnic composition from Table 7.5, page 71.*

	Your Community	New Residents (+ or -)		Butchart	Construction Workers (+ or -)	
% Under 35	_____	_____		45	100 +55%	
% Minority	_____	_____		10	30 +20%	
% Female	_____	_____		53	0 -54%	
% Race/ Ethnic origin	_____	_____		3	10 +7 (Black)	

Analysis: _____

_____

_____

_____

_____

_____

_____

_____

Test for significance: Do a Chi-Square or other statistical test for association to test the difference in demographic composition between new (either temporary or permanent) and present residents. Percentages in the above table are of total population and total new residents/and or construction workers.

CATEGORY II. COMMUNITY AND INSTITUTIONAL ARRANGEMENTS

SIA 6. Assessing the formation of attitudes toward the project from Table 8.1, page 75.

	Your Community	Acme Waste Landfill
Newspaper Articles Number & percent unfavorable	_____	3 (38%)
Public Hearing Comments Number & percent unfavorable	_____	6 (34%)
Public Opinion Survey Ratio unfavorable/favorable	_____	66%/34%
Letters from Citizens Number & percent unfavorable	_____	2 (7%)

Analysis: _____

_____

_____

Test for significance: Do a Chi-square or other test for association. If more than 35 percent of the responses are opposed, the proposed action may not receive local support.

SIA 7. Assessing interest group activity from Table 8.2, page 78.

	Your Community	Acme Waste Landfill
Groups and Organizations Percent and number unfavorable	_____	85% (17)
Estimated membership of groups and organizations Percent and number unfavorable	_____	40% (345)

Analysis:_____

_____

_____

Test for significance: Look for differences between membership numbers for favorable/unfavorable response. How large are the different organizations that are for and against the proposed action.

SIA 8. Assessing alteration in size and structure of local government from Table 8.3, page 80.

Position	Your Comm. Present	Your Comm. W/Proj	Variance (+/-)	Butchart Present	Canadian Dream Project	Variance (+/-)
Judicial/Legal	____	____	____	.25	1.0	-.75
Engineers	____	____	____	.0	.50	-.50
Admin./Managers	____	____	____	.0	1.0	-1.0
Clerical	____	____	____	1.0	1.0	0.0
Inspectors	____	____	____	1.0	2.0	-1.0
Planning	____	____	____	.0	1.0	-1.0
Public Works	____	____	____	1.0	3.0	-2.0
Assessors/Finance	____	____	____	2.0	3.5	-1.5
Regulatory	____	____	____	.0	1.0	-1.0
Other	____	____	____	____	____	____
Totals	____	____	____	5.25	14.0	-8.75

Analysis: _____

_____

_____

_____

_____

_____

_____

Test for significance: If the need is greater (or less) than three (3) local government positions you may have a significant impact. The results of this SIA variable should provide the community with a picture of the number and type of local governmental staff needed if the proposed action is permitted.

SIA 9. *Assessing presence of planning and zoning activity from Table 8.4, page 82.*

Planning and Zoning Component	Your Community Currently		Canadian Dream Currently	
	Yes	No	Yes	No
Comprehensive Plan	____	____		X
Growth Management Act	____	____		X
Zoning Laws	____	____		X
Spot Zoning Allowed	____	____	X	
Subdivision Ordinances	____	____		X
Building Codes	____	____		X
Costal Zone Regulations	____	____		X
Critical Area Ordinances	____	____		X
Wetlands Restrictions	____	____		X
Certified Planner (On staff or as consultant)	____	____		X
Other _____	____	____	____	____

Analysis: _____

Test for significance: If your community gets a lot of X's in the NO column; they may miss out on many benefits and should consider the addition of planning and zoning regulations as well as other land use controls.

SIA 10. *Assessing Industrial diversification from Table 8.5, page 84.*

	YOUR COMMUNITY			BARN-WALL		
	Number Present	Number W/Project	Variance (+/-)	Darnell Present	Darnell w/project	Variance (+/-)
Total Firms and Establishments	_____	_____	____	46	56	+10.0

Analysis: _____

Test for significance: You may collapse categories in Table 8.5 and do a statistical test of association, however, your judgment is probably best for this variable.

142

SIA 11. Assessing the Presence of living/family wage levels from Table 8.6, page 87.

Name of Business or Employer _____ (Barn-Wall is our example.)

Job Description	Project Job Numbers	Hourly Wage	Number Above Poverty	Number Part-Time	Project Job Numbers	Hourly Wage	Number Above Poverty	Number Part-Time
TOTALS	—	(Median)	—	—	104	6.50 (Median)	8[*] (7.7%)	56[**] (54%)

Analysis: _____

_____

_____

_____

_____

_____

Test for significance: You may collapse some of the categories in Table 8.6 and do statistical tests for association, although the key figure is the number of jobs that provide a family of four a living wage.

[*] In the **Barn-Wall** example, only 8 of the 104 new jobs (7.7%) provide an hourly wage above the poverty line. These numbers were current for 1997—at the time of the assessment in Darnell.

[**] 56 of the new jobs (54%) are part-time and most pay a below poverty level wage.

SIA 12. Assessing enhanced economic inequities from Table 8.7, page 89.

Your Community

	Number Unemployed	Project Job Number	Projected Number unemployed
Totals Unemployment and New Jobs	_____		_____
Percent Change (+ or -)		+ or -...	

Barn-Wall Store

	Current Number unemployed	Project Job Numbers	Projected Number unemployed
	265	104	216
			-18%

Analysis: _____

_____

_____

_____

_____

_____

_____

Test for significance: For Table 8.7 do a statistical test for proportionality between the Current Number Unemployed and Projected Number Unemployed with the proposed action. This statistical analysis assumes all project related jobs would go to those currently unemployed.

SIA 13. Assessing change in employment equity of minority groups from Table 8.8, page 92.

Your Community

	Present Number Unemployed	Project Job Numbers	Number Unemployed W/Project
Total Minority Unemployed and New Jobs	——	——	——
Percent Change (+ or -)			(·········)

Barn-Wall Store

	Current Number Unemployed	Employee Numbers	Number Unemployed W/Project
Total Minority Unemployed and New Jobs	145	104	120
Percent Change (+ or -)			-17%

Analysis: _____

_____

_____

_____

_____

_____

Test for Significance: For Table 8.8 do a statistical test for association between the current number of unemployed minorities and projected number of unemployed minorities with the proposed action. This statistical analysis assumes all project related jobs would go to currently unemployed minorities.

SIA 14. Assessing Changing Occupational Opportunities from Table 8.9, page 95.

Job Category	Your Community			Barn-Wall Store		
	Current Number Employed	Project Job Numbers	Percent Change (+ or -)	Current Number Employed	Project Job Numbers	Percent Change (+ or -)
------------ (ex. Clerical/Sales)	_____	_____	_____	190	70	+37
------------ (ex. Maids/Janitors)	_____	_____	_____	28	6	+21
------------	---------	---------	---------	xxx	xxx	xxx
------------	---------	---------	---------	xxx	xxx	xxx
------------	---------	---------	---------	xxx	xxx	xxx
------------	---------	---------	---------			
Total Change in Job Numbers	_____	_____		1,291	104	+8.1

Analysis: _____

_____

Test for significance: For Table 8.9 do a statistical test for association between the current number of job holders in each category and projected number in each category with the proposed action. However, if you wish focus on the percent changes for each occupational category.

CATEGORY III. COMMUNITIES IN TRANSITION

SIA 15. Assessing the Presence of Outside Agency from Table 9.1, page 99.

	Your Community	**Acme Waste**
Will the proposed action bring an outside agency or organization to your community?	_____	Yes

Analysis: _____

_____

_____

_____

Test for significance: This is an "either-or" SIA variable. Caution: There may be more than one outside agency.

SIA 16. Assessing the Level of Inter-Organizational Cooperation from Table 9.2, Page 101.

	Your Community	**Canadian Dream**
Total number of permits, consultations and approvals required before going ahead	_____	16

Analysis: _____

_____

_____

_____

Test for significance: Look for more than four (4) levels of approval and the possible need for additional consultation.

SIA 17. Assessing The Introduction Of New Social Classes From Table 9.4, page 105.

Job Category	Your Community			Barn-Wall Store		
	Percent Presently Employed	Percent Employed w/wo Project	Change (+/-)	Percent Presently Employed	Percent Employed w/wo Project	Change (+/-)
(Farm Operators)	___	___	___	29	27	-2
(Clerical/Sales)	___	___	___	15	19	+4
(Craftsman/Foreman)	___	___	___	7	6	-1
___	___	___	___			
___	___	___	___			

Analysis: _____

_____

_____

_____

_____

Test for significance: Statistical tests for association could be done using the occupational categories where there was change if there are at least four cells. However, your explanations should focus on explaining the type of occupations that will likely change.

SIA 18. Assessing Change in the Commercial/Industrial Focus of the Community from Table 9.5 and 9.6, page 107.

Community	**Present** **Present Classification**	**Projected** **Projected Classification**
Acme Waste Management	agriculture (rural)	rural diversified (garbage town)
Your Community (from census labels)	_____	_____
Your Community (from needs assessment)	_____	_____

Analysis: _____

_____

Test for significance: Based on the evaluation and experience of the SIA practitioner.

SIA 19. Assessing the Presence of Weekend Residents and Short Term Visitors from Table 9.7, page 109.

	Your Community	**Canadian Dream**
Current Population	_____	4,700
Number Weekend Residents	_____	800
Percent Change (+ or -)	_____	+17%
Accommodations for Weekend Residents	_____	25

Analysis: _____

_____

_____

Test for significance: Look for increases or decreases of plus or minus 5 percent from the resident population. Lack of overnight accommodation is indicative of an infrastructure need. It also suggests that not all the benefits of the proposed action are being captured by the local community.

CATEGORY IV. INDIVIDUAL AND FAMILY LEVEL IMPACTS

SIA 20. Assessing the Disruption in Daily Living and Movement Patterns from Table 10.1, page 113.

Type of Disruption	Your Community Yes	Your Community No	Acme Waste Yes	Acme Waste No
Increased noise	_____	_____	X	
Foul or unusual odors	_____	_____		X
Increased air pollution	_____	_____	X	
Dust and commotion	_____	_____	X	
Increased vehicular traffic	_____	_____	X	
Visual Alteration	_____	_____	X	
Polluted waters	_____	_____		?
Closed roads and bridges	_____	_____	X	
Disruption of utilities	_____	_____	X	
Other temporary closures	_____	_____	?	
Nuclear contamination	_____	_____		X
Other _____	_____	_____	_____	_____

Analysis: _____

_____

_____

_____

Test for significance: There are no significant thresholds for disruptions as each one could be considered important by a segment of the impacted community. Report the number and type of disruption and use the findings for discussion during the mitigation process.

SIA 21. *Assessing the Dissimilarity in Religious and Cultural Practices from Table 10.2, page 115.*

	Your Community		**Acme Waste**	
	Present	Projected	Present	Projected
Presence of Distinct Cultural/ Religious groups	_____	_____	No	No

Analysis: _____

_____

_____

Test for significance: A present or absent SIA variable.

SIA 22. *Alterations in Family Structure from Table 10.3, page 117.*

For Persons over 18 years	**Your Community**			**Acme Waste**		
	Present	**Newcomers**	Percent +/-	**Present**	**Newcomers**	Percent +/-
% Married	_____	_____	_____	65	50	-15
% Never Married	_____	_____	_____	10	40	+30
% Divorced	_____	_____	_____	5	10	+5
% Widow(er)	_____	_____	_____	20	0	-20

Analysis: _____

_____

_____

_____

Test for significance: If you have at least four cells with differences, do a statistical test for association.

SIA 23. Assessing the Disruption of Social Networks from Table 10.4, page 118.

	Your Community	**Canadian Dream**
Number Households Affected	_____	40
% of Households Low Income?	_____	15
% of Households Racial, Ethnic and/or Native?	_____	None
% of Households over 65?	_____	20
% of Households with Distinct Religious or Cultural groups?	_____	None

Analysis: _____

_____

_____

_____

_____

_____

_____

_____

_____

Test for significance: Do a statistical test for association if there are compositional differences in the impacted households.

SIA 24. Assessing the Perceptions of Public Health and Safety from Table 10.5, page 120

Health and Safety Issue	Your Community No	Your Community Yes	Acme Waste No	Acme Waste Yes
Air pollution and dust	____	____		X
Noise levels	____	____	X	
Nuclear fallout	____	____	X	X
Vehicular accidents	____	____		X
Odors and smells	____	____		X
Environmental degradation	____	____		X
Surface water pollution	____	____		X
Groundwater contamination	____	____		X
Drinking water contamination	____	____		X
Other_____	____	____	--	
Other_____	____	____	--	

Analysis: _____

_____

_____

_____

_____

Test of significance: Each issue could be significant depending upon the proposed action, so each needs to be reported and verified by data from a variety of sources including the project proponent.

SIA 25. Assessing the Change in Leisure Opportunities from Table 10.6, page 122.

Leisure Opportunity	Present Situation	With Development	Present Situation	Canadian Dream
Swimming pools	_____	_____	No	Yes
Boating areas	_____	_____	No	Yes
Camping sites	_____	_____	No	No
Playgrounds	_____	_____	No	No
Picnic tables	_____	_____	No	Yes
Fishing ponds	_____	_____	Yes	Yes
Golf courses	_____	_____	No	No
Tennis courts	_____	_____	No	Yes
Nature center	_____	_____	No	No
Youth center	_____	_____	No	No
Senior center	_____	_____	No	No
Miles (Km) of Walking paths	_____	_____	None	10km
Miles (km) of Bike paths	_____	_____	None	12km
Other Facilities	_____	_____	_____	_____

Analysis: _____

_____

_____

_____

Test of significance: No statistical test are available, however by completing Table 10.6 the community will have a good picture of needed leisure and recreation facilities. If available during the baseline study, use levels of service or standards to determine if recreation and leisure opportunities are adequate, both before and after the proposed action is implemented.

CATEGORY V. COMMUNITY INFRASTRUCTURE NEEDS

SIA 26. Assessing the Change in Community Infrastructure from Table 11.1, Page 128.

Community Infrastructure	Your Community			Present Situation	Barn-Wall	
	Present Situation	Number with Project	Variance (+ or -)		Darnell Number Required	Variance (+ or -)
Police/Sheriffs (2.1)	___	___	___	3.5	7.8	-4.3
Patrol Cars (1.1)	___	___	___	2	4.1	-2.3
Firefighters (1.5)	___	___	___	4.5	5.5	-1.0
Medic Units (.25)	___	___	___	0	0.9	-0.9
Hospital Beds (3.3)	___	___	___	10	12.2	-2.2
Physicians (.9)	___	___	___	1	3.3	-2.3
Dentists (.8)	___	___	___	1	3.0	-2.0
Nurses (.7)	___	___	___	2	2.6	-0.6
Certified Teachers (4.8)	___	___	___	15	17.7	-2.7
Adult/juvenile detention (3.6)*	___	___	___	9	13.3	-4.3
Libraries (700 sq. ft.)*	___	___	___	1	1.0	0.0
Acres of parkland (10.0)	___	___	___	12	37.0	-25.0
Acres of open space (12.5)	___	___	___	25	46.2	-21.2
Linear trails in miles (1.0)	___	___	___	3	3.7	-0.7
Totals	___		(+ or -)		Totals =	-69.5

Rates expressed per 1,000 persons. For a population of 3,700 the multiplier is 3.7. Detention facilities expressed in beds and library space in square feet.

154

Analysis of Community Infrastructure Needs

_____

_____

_____

_____

_____

_____

_____

_____

_____

_____

_____

_____

_____

_____

_____

_____

Test for Significance: A Chi-Square or other tests for association could be done comparing facilities with and without the project. However, the deficiencies or excess in community infrastructure should be used in the mitigation and enhancement process. Completing Table 11.1 will provide citizens and community leaders a good picture of community needs.

SIA 27. Assessing Land Acquisition and Disposal from Table 11.2, page 131.

	Your Community	**Acme Waste**
Private or Public (current/proposed)	_____	Private to Private
Assessed Property Evaluation (change in value and in percent)	_____ (new value)	+4,820,000
	_____ (percent change)	(+2,678%)
Estimated Sales Tax Revenue	_____	Not Available

Analysis: _____

_____

_____

Test for significance: If the assessed value increases by at least 50 percent, the added or lost revenue will have an impact on services provided by the local governmental unit.

SIA 28. Assessing the Effects on Known Cultural, Historical, Sacred and Archaeological Resources From Table 11.3, page 133.

Resource	Your Community Yes	No	Barn-Wall Yes	No
Registered Historical Site (e.g. National Historic Register)	___	___		X
Certified Archeological Site	___	___		X
Sacred or Spiritual Places	___	___		X
Cemeteries/Graves	___	___		X
State/County/Local Park	___	___		X
Proposed Historical Site Listing	___	___		X
Other_____	___	___		

Analysis:_____

Test for significance: This is a presence or absence variable. If you checked yes to any item, it will need to be reviewed prior to project approval. Some mitigation/ and or approval may be required by the appropriate authority!

Activity 12.1   Ranking Social Impacts for Your Community

Instructions: To this point in Chapter 12 you have entered the data for those SIA variables which you have found to be significant, and explained *why* each variable is significant. In this activity, based on your judgment and other members of the assessment team, select the most significant SIA variables and rank them from (1) to (12) for the community you are assessing. Remember, the goal is to select the most important variables for *your community*, using the example of the **Acme Waste Management** landfill as shown in Figure 12.1 below enter your selection in Table 12.1 on page 158.

Figure 12.1
Social Impact Assessment Variables Ranked from One through Twelve
for the Acme Waste Management Landfill

Rank	Variable	SIA#
1.	Formation of attitudes	(#6)
2.	Interest group activity	(#7)
3.	Perceptions of public health and safety	(#24)
4.	Presence of outside agency	(#15)
5.	Relocation of individuals and families	(#4)
6.	Change in commercial focus of community	(#18)
7.	Influx of temporary workers	(#2)
8.	Presence of zoning and planning	(#6)
9.	Industrial diversification	(#10)
10.	Disruptions of daily living patterns	(#23)
11.	Change in community infrastructure	(#26)
12.	Land acquisition and/or disposal	(#27)

Step 1. Enter the SIA variable labels and numbers in Table 12.1 for your assessment.

Ranking of Social Impact Assessment Variables for Your Assessment

Rank	Variable	SIA#
1.		
2.		
3.		
4.		
5.		
6.		
7.		
8.		
9.		
10.		
11.		
12.		

Now that you have decided what is important and have the data to support it—you can begin to develop the mitigation and monitoring process.

Proceed to Chapter 13.

Chapter 13. Mitigation, Monitoring and a Social Impact Management Plan (SIMP)

In Chapter 12, you summarized and provided a written description of the social impacts that are likely to occur as a result of a project or policy change (the proposed action). In the mitigation/enhancement/monitoring step of the SIA process you will focus on enhancing benefits and minimizing any negative consequences. The suggested procedures for mitigation and monitoring of identified significant social impacts are included in the suggested outline for a Social Impact Management Plan (SIMP) at the end of this chapter.

Enhancement is not included in the original NEPA legislation or in the U.S. Council on Environmental Quality guidelines, nor in Environmental Impact Assessment guidelines in other parts of the world. Change has many positive features which may "enhance" the quality of life for both individuals and communities. At the same time we need to insure that the biophysical systems that support human systems are not degraded. For example, a properly constructed and monitored landfill is preferable to one which might leak and contaminate public drinking sources. Planners, community leaders, private citizens, as well as the business and industrial community must look upon change as a way of improving life in their community and continuing a profitable business sector.

First a mitigation strategy

➡

Activity 13.1 The SIA Mitigation Strategy

Definition: The mitigation strategy detailed in this *Guide* to manage community and regional level social impacts (Figure 13.1) comes from the U.S. National Environmental Policy Act (NEPA) of 1970 and is widely followed by U.S. federal and state agencies (e.g., U.S. Army Corps of Engineers-Environmental Protection Agency, 1991; *Economic and Social Analysis*, U.S. Forest Service Handbook, 1909.17, Section 35.9 and 37.21, August 1985.)

A mitigation strategy as followed by the U.S. Forest Service may be summarized using the example of a proposed ski resort in Southern Oregon.

1. In the first step, the forest supervisor attempts to **avoid** all identified adverse social and biophysical impacts.
2. In the second step, alternative designs are proposed which **minimize** any adverse impacts on soil and vegetation.
3. In the **compensation** step, the proponent is responsible for undertaking activity to deal with soil and vegetation loss both on site and elsewhere.

Compensation for the loss of vegetation, for example, could be to acquire other sites, pay for present and future revenue losses to the Forest Service or enhance a degraded site. The amount of compensation can be based on the quality and type of forest cover, the severity of the impact and tradeoff between development and natural scenery. Financial compensation may not apply to all social impacts, as it does to soil runoff and timber loss, but opportunities to enhance other social and recreational values may be present.

A mitigation strategy can be applied to the adverse significant impacts associated with any stage in the SIA process—planning, construction, operation and maintenance or decommissioning—to determine which can be avoided or minimized (Chapters 3 and 4).

Instructions: The first two steps of mitigation—**avoiding** and **minimizing**—can apply both to the project itself and to the host community. For example, elements of the proposed ski project may be revised to avoid or minimize adverse social impacts, or the community may be able to take steps to attenuate, if not avoid, any adverse effects. For more information on mitigation see:
📖 *Concepts,* Chapters 7 and 15.

Application of a strategy for mitigation of adverse social impacts requires that the assessor first rank the level of importance of each identified significant SIA variable. This step is illustrated for **Acme Waste Management** in Table 13.1, which was taken from Table 12.2, page 157 in the previous chapter.

Table 13.1
Significant Social Impact Assessment Variables Ranked from One through Twelve
for the Acme Waste Management Landfill, From Chapter 12, page 157

Rank	Variable	SIA#
1.	Formation of attitudes	(#6)
2.	Interest group activity	(#7)
3.	Perceptions of public health and safety	(#24)
4.	Presence of outside agency	(#15)
5.	Relocation of individuals and families	(#4)
6.	Change in commercial focus of community	(#18)
7.	Influx of temporary workers	(#2)
8.	Presence of zoning and planning	(#6)
9.	Industrial diversification	(#10)
10.	Disruptions of daily living patterns	(#23)
11.	Change in community infrastructure	(#26)
12.	Change in land ownership	(#27)

Step 1. Avoid Adverse Effects
The first step in evaluating possible mitigation strategies for each SIA variable is to determine whether the proponent could revise the proposed action to **avoid adverse effects**. For example, to address the problems associated with relocating of the 26 families, the assessor might recommend **Acme Waste Management** pay for a new home and assist in moving.

> …to enhance benefits, the community must be an active participant during the mitigation and enhancement step

The project proponents or community social agencies might help persons find homes, arrange for moving, and otherwise help in adjusting to their new surroundings (relocation of individuals and families). The main route proposed to reach the landfill in Arvana, will require extensive upgrading to accommodate large trucks. Upgrading will result in closing the road and requiring the residents to drive out of their way to leave a large subdivision (disruption of daily living patterns). The main road goes between the hospital and the high school, raising concerns about the safety of older and handicapped persons and aesthetic issues resulting from the use of this road for hauling waste (perceptions of public health and safety). Each of these issues could be addressed by relocating the route one mile to the South. That road would have to be rebuilt, but would only disrupt a few residents.
Make a blank copy and complete table 13.1 for your project with suggestions for avoiding adverse identified impacts for the proposed action.

Figure 13.1
Mitigation Components for Identified Social Impacts
(A Mitigation/Monitoring Strategy Based on the NEPA Process)[1]

From List of Significant Social Impact Variables
For Acme Waste Management Shown in Chapter 12, page 157

Ways to **Avoid** Social Impacts		Ways to **Minimize** Social Impacts		Ways to **Rectify** Social Impacts		Ways to **Reduce** Social Impacts		**Unresolved** Social Impacts	
Community	Proponent	Community	Proponent	Community	Proponent	Community	Proponent	Compensation	Public Involvement

Data for Monitoring Social Impacts

List **SIA** Variables	Establish **Monitoring** Responsibilities

[1] **Source:** National Environmental Policy Act of 1969 (NEPA), Section 102, c(v). Pub. L. 91-190, 42 USC, 4321-4347, January 1, 1970, as amended by Pub. L. 94-52, July 3, 1975, and Pub. L. 94-83, August 9, 1975, and Council on Environmental Quality, "Regulations for Implementing the Procedural Provision of National Environmental Policy Act," 40 CFR, 1508-20, July 1, 1986.

Step 2. Minimize Adverse Effects

> Government Officials could avoid future problems in developing community infrastructure by providing a statement of needed improvements to the project proponent and the appropriate municipality or regional authority

The next step in mitigation is to identify ways to **minimize** adverse social impacts. For example, three of the social impacts, (formation of attitudes toward the project, perceptions of public health and safety, and presence of an outside agency), shown in Table 13.1, could be addressed with joint proponent, community-sponsored education programs. Attitudes (particularly negative ones) formed about the landfill, cannot be eliminated, but can be dealt with, if the public has complete information about the proposed project. If the public is aware of both benefits *and* possible consequences of a proposal, and given an opportunity to participate in resolving the issues, there is likely to be less hostility than if information is withheld under the false hope that controversy will be avoided.

Acme Waste Management in collaboration with the host community could, therefore, begin a campaign to inform the public of the contributions and the benefits of the project. Proposals for rerouting to minimize traffic congestion during construction could be the subject of a news article in the local paper. Such an approach would make it easier for **Acme Waste Management**, an outside private sector business, to begin the process of becoming part of the community.

As a procedure to minimize social impacts the community could also begin an education program to discuss any health consequences that might exist with the waste disposal facility. That action might reduce any negative attitudes formed about the project and allay some of the negative perceptions. Community leaders could initiate monitoring by forming a citizens' group to address problems that may arise from the start of construction to the closing of the facility in approximately 40 years. Such a program would give residents a voice in the decision making process and minimize interest group activity and moderate negative attitudes that greet all waste siting activity (the NIMBY syndrome).

Step 3. Instructions for Table 13.2.

Expand the worksheet to include all identified significant variables from Table 13.1 followed by suggestions to Avoid, Minimize and Reduce each identified social impact.

Table 13.2 Suggested Procedures for Avoiding, Minimizing and Reducing the Significant Social Impacts Using the Acme Waste Management Landfill as our example.

Significant SIA Variable	Proponent to Avoid Impacts	Community to Avoid Impacts	Proponent to Minimize Impacts	Community to Minimize Impacts	Proponent to Reduce Impacts	Community to Reduce Impacts
Perception of Public Health & Safety	Educational Program	Educational Program	Educational Program	Educational Program	Educational Program	Educational Program
Relocation of Families/ Individuals	Pay for relocation	Social Services Assistance	???????	Locate comparable homes	....	....
Lack zoning regulations	....	Implement Planning and zoning	???????	Benefits of zoning regulations	???????	???????
Disrupt Living Patterns	Change route to landfill	Approve new routes to landfill	???????	Facilitate building new route	???????	???????
Change in Land Ownership	Provide property valuations	Assess for new tax evaluation	Request Change in zoning	Zone with special use permit	Equitable fee schedule	Phase in new taxes
Expand rows for significant variables	....	....	....	....	....	....
Expand rows for all significant variables	....	....	....	....	....	....

Activity 13.2 Identifying Data Sources for Community Monitoring

The next activity for your **Social Impact Assessment** is monitoring the significant social impacts. *Monitoring* is a long-term process of making sure the mitigation procedures for the social impacts you identified are actually being carried out. Go back to that portion of each chapter where the data sources are listed for your most significant variables. Enter these data sources, including the page number from the **Guide,** in Table 13.2. Next, list the agency or organization with monitoring responsibility. Example responsible units might include the city/municipality planning department, the county or regional planning office or monitoring might involve a state or provincial agency. Next, enter a date when the first data collection or monitoring should take place. Finally, make sure your SIA report is on file with the local library, the appropriate administrative agency and the local planning office. An example is shown in the first row of Table 13.3 below.

Your Project: _____

Monitoring Agency or Citizen Oversight committee to Supervise Monitoring: _____

_____

Table 13.3 Identification of Data Sources, Monitoring, Responsibility and Frequency for Monitoring activity

Social Impact Assessment Variables	Data Sources for Monitoring	Monitoring Responsibility	Monitoring Frequency
(Relocation of families and individuals)	(Number of families and individuals moved when landfill was built)	(Project proponent and local social services agency)	(Should be done yearly until relocation is satisfactory)
Formationof Attitudes Toward Project	(Public Opinion Surveys and discussion in Public media—Chapter 8.	Project Proponent and Citizen Advisory Committee	Done bi-monthly until community acceptance
Perceptions of Public Health and Safety	(Public Opinion Surveys and discussion on Public media Chapter 8	Project Proponent and Citizen Advisory Committee	Done bi-monthly until community acceptance
…………………...	………………………	……………………………	……………………
…………………...	………………………	……………………………	……………………

Activity 13.3 Developing and Presenting Project Modification Alternatives and Suggestions for Community Adaptation as Part of a Social Impact Management Plan

Objectives:

The objectives of this activity are to help you use the knowledge and data you have acquired:

1. To develop suggestions for resolving any conflicts which may arise because of issues associated with the proposed project or policy change; and
2. To begin to develop a plan of action for maximizing those positive benefits which may accrue to your community if the proposed action is implemented.

Instructions:

Use the information in Chapter 12, *Putting it all Together*, and information you collected for each of the 28 SIA variables to develop recommendations for mitigating and/or enhancing the outcomes of the proposal for which you are doing an SIA. Both as a summary and a help to you, complete Table 13.4 for the most important social impact assessment variables (use Table 13.2 as a guide). These abbreviated responses will help you communicate the results of your effort to others. Depending upon the proposed action, you may extend your mitigation/enhancement activity to all significant SIA variables.

Step 1.   Development Recommendations for *Project Modification* for proponent.

Variable...

1. _____

_____

_____

2. _____

_____

_____

3. _____

_____

_____

4. _____

_____

_____

Step 2. Developing Recommendations to the *Host Community* for adapting to the proposed changes.

Variable...

1. _____

_____

2. _____

_____

_____

3. _____

_____

Step 4. Complete Table 13.4 for each identified significant SIA variable

Table 13.4 Summary of Suggested Project Modifications and Recommendations for Community Adaptation to Change and Listing of SIA Variables that May Lead to Unavoidable Change

Social Impact Assessment Variables	Project Modification	Community Action	Unavoidable Changes
1. Formation of attitudes toward the project	_____	_____	Yes
2. Interest group activity	_____	_____	Yes
6. Change in commercial focus of the community	_____	_____	Yes
7. Influx of temporary workers	_____	_____	Yes
9. Industrial diversification	_____	_____	Yes

Given the range of stakeholders involved in projects and the complexity of some social issues, it is not always possible to reach full agreement, consensus or a clear way forward on all mitigation strategies at the time a final SIMP is submitted with the joint SIA-EIS. Where there are unresolved matters, actions to resolve these matters should be articulated and included in the mitigation table of the final plan as shown on p. 165 of chapter 13 and listed in the space below. In such cases, a working copy of the plan should be submitted with the final EIS and should contain the actions needed to resolve issues and to develop mitigation strategies. The actions nominated to resolve issues should be accompanied by progress measures and time frames in the monitoring plan, and be reported as project implementation proceeds. It is impossible to resolve every issue. However, if the proponent and the impacted community are aware of the key issues and each is addressed in the appropriate public forum, progress toward eventual reconciliation may occur.

Activity 13.4 SIA Final Summary

The last section should provide a concise summary of the project, that includes information developed from the social impact assessment that summarizes key mitigation strategies and initiatives. The following should be considered for inclusion if required as the SIA may either be a standalone report or include other assessment components:[1]

- Name and location of the project
- Brief project summary including the project's objectives and expected outcomes
- A description of the project's social and cultural zone of influence
- Key social and cultural impact issues identified in the completed SIA
- An overview of the public involvement program and SIA stakeholder engagement strategy including key stakeholders and community issues and concerns identified during the scoping process
- Key mitigation measures and benefit strategies proposed including positive and negative impacts to the proponent and the community
- SIA monitoring processes
- The final SIA along with the EIA should be attached.

Activity 13.5 Outlining a Social Impact Management Plan (SIMP)

At this point in the assessment process, the Social Impact Assessor has completed all the components needed to develop a Social Impact Management Plan (SIMP) if required by the proponent and/or the licensing agency.

Note 1: A Social Impact Management Plan (SIMP)
A social impact management plan establishes the roles and responsibilities of proponents, Provincial, Municipal and Federal governments, First Nations, other stakeholders and communities throughout the life of a project, by managing social impacts and opportunities during construction, operation and maintenance and decommissioning. You must have completed the social impact assessment of the proposed action as detailed in all previous chapters of the *Guide.*

Note 2: What Should A Social Impact Management Plan Contain?

At a minimum, the social impact management plan should include:
- An overall summary of the completed or proposed action.
- The completed SIA and EIA.
- The mitigation monitoring and management strategies included in this chapter.
- The public involvement and stakeholder engagement strategies
- Dispute resolution process between proponent and the community.

> ## Caution: A Social Impact Management Plan (SIMP) requires a completed SIA and EIA.

Note 3: When Are Social Impact Management Plans Required?

A social impact management plan is required for either new or expanded major resource development projects which require an environmental impact statement (EIS) to be prepared under the legislative requirements of the impacted Province or Territory. In addition, it may be required for the Impacts and Benefits Agreements (Chapter 14) between a proponent and a legal authority such as a First Nation and as part of or in addition to a Socio-Economic Participation Agreement (SEPA).

Ideally, proponents should submit a draft social impact management plan following the completion of the SIA and EIA, and submit the plan to the appropriate permitting agency and the Indigenous, First Nation, Municipality, or appropriate civil government administration. A final plan reflecting the outcomes of consultation with effected governments should then be submitted with the final SIS-EIS.

Note 4: Who Is Responsible For Preparing A Social Impact Management Plan?

The proponent (and in many cases, this means you the social impact assessor), is responsible. In preparing the plan, the proponent must collaborate with stakeholders, to include not only the proponent, but the impacted community, relevant government agencies and affected indigenous populations and other stakeholders identified during the scoping process. Information may be obtained from the section on stakeholder identification under Scoping in Chapter 4. A **Citizens Advisory Board or Monitoring Board** could ensure that the mitigation procedures that were identified in the mitigation and monitoring (Chapter 13) are actually being carried out. List below the expected composition of the Monitoring Board and who will respond to the findings and recommendations of a Citizen Member Advisory type board. See table on page 41 for example stakeholders.

Note 5: Social Impact Management Plan Dispute Resolution

The dispute resolution mechanism for the social impact management plan should support an active response to community and stakeholder concerns about social impact issues. In most instances, proponents have well established policies, procedures and mechanisms to respond to disputes, grievances and complaints. The social impact management plan dispute resolution may be aligned to these existing organizational processes or included in the socio-economic participation agreement (SEPA) as outlined in Chapter 14.

In the space below enter the permitting governmental authority and if available, the link to the SIMP requirements for that authority.

Requirement for SIMP:_____

Link: _____

If the permitting agency or the project promoter does not have a requirement for a social impact management plan, the recommendations for modifications in the proposal and recommendations to the community constitutes the end of your SIA. **1**

---

[1] A portion of this chapter draws upon a publication by the Queensland, Australia Department of Infrastructure and Planning in cooperation with the Queensland Resources Council and the Local Government Association of Queensland titled *Guideline to Preparing a Social Impact Management Plan*. http://www.dsdip.qld.gov.au/resources/guideline/simp-guideline.pdf portions of that document used here with permission of the publisher. © State of Queensland. Published by the Department of Infrastructure and Planning, September 2010, 100 George Street, Brisbane Qld 4000.

As a substitute for a SIMP, a Socio-Economic Participation Agreement (SEPA) pursuant to a Memorandum of Understanding (MOU) may be entered into on a supra (extra) legal basis between proponents of mining projects and First Nations in certain Canadian Provinces The MOU applies during exploration and at the start of production both parties would develop a Socio-Economic Participation Agreement (SEPA) to apply to the remaining Phases of the Mining Project (Chapter 15, page 198). The Socio-Economic Partnership Agreement does include a provision for dispute resolution but now external enforcement is available

Chapter 14 deals with types of Impacts and benefits agreements that may be entered into between the proponent and the impacted community.

Chapter 14. Impacts and Benefits Agreement

What are Impacts and Benefits Type of Agreements (IBAs)?

IBAs are essentially supra-regulatory tools meant to address impacts from natural resource developments and ensure that benefits are delivered, in particular, to Aboriginal and Indigenous communities proximate to and impacted by natural resource developments. Agreements are about what benefits can be expected and about impact monitoring and mitigation. Benefits and Impacts are often thought of together, but they are two different, but complimentary processes.

Canada is one country that specifically encourages an IBA between companies that apply for mineral development that involve Indigenous or First Nation land ownership or claims in the three Northern Territories and the Provinces of British Columbia and Alberta. Notwithstanding an absence of specific legislation requiring their use; in recent decades a number of Impact and Benefit Agreements (IBAs) have been established between mining firms and Aboriginal communities in support of similar projects across northern Canada. These negotiated, private agreements serve to document in a contractual form the benefits that a local community can expect from the development of natural resources in exchange for its support and cooperation. Their specific content varies, but typically they include provisions on royalties and/or profit-sharing, employment, wider economic development opportunities, and enhanced protection of environmental and socio-cultural amenities.

IBAs are noteworthy for two reasons. First, they provide some assurances to, and tangible benefits for, local communities facing a major natural resource development, such as a gold mine, in a way that conventional regulatory mechanisms like environmental impact assessment have never been able to provide. Second, they have largely been established without the explicit involvement of the provincial, state or federal government, that retain traditional sovereign authority in all matters of natural resource allocation and development.

In the State of Western Australia and the Australian Northern Territory, proponents of the more contentious mining, oil and gas projects do make contracts with traditional (Aboriginal) land owners (⇾O'Faircheallaigh, 1999). However, the Western Australia Environmental Protection Agency specifically avoids IBAs and uses mitigation for approving permits. In the Australian State of Queensland, they rely upon a Social Impact Management Plan (SIMP) as the basis for detailing benefits agreements (Chapter13). In European Union Countries, benefit agreements are included in the Environmental and Social Action Plans with the focus on monitoring social impacts in progress. The European Bank for Reconstruction and Development (EBRD) follows the procedures and regulations of the European Union.

The Republic of South Africa explicitly requires a social development output for mineral development in the form of a Social Labour Plan enforced by the Department of Mineral Resources. The South African Plan is for both operation and decommissioning impacts. The World Bank does not have specific requirements for IBA's, rather they have policies to ensure the environmental and social soundness and sustainability of investment projects and integration of social aspects of projects during the decision-making process. The Bank's policy is to minimize involuntary resettlement and implement projects that fosters full respect for indigenous people's dignity, human rights, and cultural uniqueness. The World Bank develops IBAs in response to particular socio-economic contexts with guidance of current safeguards policies.

Labels by which Impact and Benefit Agreements are Known

The names vary widely depending upon the specific purpose, however, almost all refer to a formal or informal agreement between a project proponent, be it private sector industry or a governmental entity, and a host community, region or nation that is a legal entity such as a First Nation or a community with a collective identity. A selection of different labels include:

- *Impact Benefits Agreement* is used to refer to a legal requirement for the three Northern Territories and other Provinces of Canada when permits for natural resource development (generally mineral extraction) are requested on First Nation lands. The requirement applies for exploration, transportation and extraction on First Nation land claims.

- *Socio-Economic Plan Document* refers to mitigation requirements after social and financial impacts have been identified (similar to a SIMP). These can include mechanisms to enhance benefits to impacted populations.

- *Approval with Mitigation (SEPA-U.S.):* for the several U.S. states that have NEPA style legislation, projects are generally approved when the proponent has met or agreed to required mitigation.

- *Memorandum of Understanding* are formal (sometimes informal) agreements between the proponent and the impacted community for identified mitigation measures. Generally used during the exploration phase prior to the licensing application (AIR-Application Information Requirements or TOR-Terms of Reference).

- *Socio-Economic Mitigation Agreement* means the proponent agrees to particular measures, for example, to reserve certain job and business spin-off opportunities for persons living in the impacted area.

- *Revenue Sharing Agreements* deal with the sharing of royalties among governmental and quasi-governmental units to include the impacted communities.

- *Community Benefits Agreement* is another name for the IBA covering financial and general infrastructure benefits for the host community, including social infrastructure.

- *Resettlement Action Plans (RAP)* is normally a requirement of local and international lending agencies if large numbers of persons are to be involuntarily relocated.

- *The Social and Labour Plan* is used in South Africa to refer to pre- as well as post-project requirements under the Mineral and Petroleum Resources Development Act dealing with identified social impacts.

- *Project Labor Agreements* generally means the project proponent is required to hire a certain percentage of local labor during the construction and operation phase and may require the purchase of materials and supplies from local vendors.

- *Development Agreements--City and Municipal* Examples would be International Olympic type events where athlete housing is required and the municipal unit provides financial backing as a condition for accepting the units when the event is over. Many urban areas have similar arrangements for the construction of low-income housing.

- Several international mining corporations use a *Community Development Management Plan* (similar to a SIMP) as the basis to make a contribution to the livelihoods of people in the impacted communities. A social baseline study provides data for the plan. These management plans are developed to ensure that the company's license to operate is enhanced and maintained.

- *Conditions on a Consent* are applied in some jurisdictions , such as New Zealand, and these can include local environmental enhancement, social infrastructure, training and employment plans and community trust funds for local enhancement projects.

Activity 14.1 A Brief History of Impacts and Benefits Agreements (IBAs) in Canada

IBAs were first negotiated in the mid seventies between the Canadian federal or provincial government and a project proponent as part of Aboriginal land claim settlements. The government would attempt to gain financial benefits for the local community and to mitigate the negative social and cultural impacts on their traditional lifestyle. The policy of the Canadian government, at the time, was to develop employment opportunities for Indigenous populations through private sector activity. Since the 1990s, IBAs have been negotiated by the impacted communities themselves--for several important reasons.

First, there is a growing legal recognition of Aboriginal rights established through treaties, land claim agreements and Aboriginal court challenges.

As a result of the comprehensive 1984 Inuvialuit agreement in Northern Canada, industry must consult with Aboriginal peoples if they wish to construct and operate a pipeline to cross Inuvialuit lands to reach non-Inuvialuit lands. In return for the use of lands, industry may have to reimburse "costs associated with any Inuvialuit Land Administration inspection of the development works sites and the nature and scope of such inspection; wildlife compensation, restoration and mitigation; employment, service and supply contracts; education and training; and equity participation or other types of participatory benefits." (← (Kerr, 2000 and Kennett, 1999 and Campbell, Singliner and Johnston, 2001)

A second reason is a growing desire among Indigenous and Aboriginal groups to participate in negotiations with industry to mitigate the negative impacts of resource development and to use it as a tool for community economic development.

First Nations have shown a growing interest in playing an active part in financial and economic developments, shifting from passive acceptance of low skill, short-term employment to becoming masters of their own house and insisting upon partnerships that result in sharing of long-term benefits with an emphasis on career employment opportunities.

__Finally__, the trend is for private sector companies as a legal entity to consult directly with Aboriginal groups.

Natural resource developers (to include mining companies) have moved outside their traditional roles as profit-oriented business ventures into a quasi-public sector role of supporting short and long term social and financial benefits. "The mineral industry is recognizing that a special situation exists when exploring in Traditional Aboriginal and Indigenous Lands and is adapting business practices to reduce negative impacts and increase social and economic opportunities for northern communities."

Activity 14.2 Developing the Impacts and Benefits Agreement

The following list the IBA elements and the mitigated social impacts to consider for your project. Many of the social impacts are included in your now completed SIA. Additional items may be added depending upon legal requirements and directives from the proponent's parent organization. IBAs have evolved from being narrow in scope and focused only on employment, training and business opportunities to being much broader instruments of socio-economic development that include a range of provisions like for example fixed cash payments and environmental protection among others. (Steven Kenneth, 1999). You may tap into an Impact Benefit Agreement research network at http://www.impactandbenefit.com

Step 1. **Introductory Provisions.** Introductory provisions describe the context for the agreements and set out the basis for the ongoing relationship between the impacted community and the proponent. Standard contractual elements include protocols such as preambles, definitions, purpose sections and introductory provisions. Many law firms in major Canadian Cities have example First Nation Mineral Exploration and Development Protocols. Enter possible protocols for your project in the space below (with additional sheets as necessary):

Preambles and details on proposed project locations……………………………..

………………………………………………………………………………………..

Definition of Terms in plain language…………………………………………….

………………………………………………………………………………………..

Step 2. **Provisions to encourage employment and provide training to local communities**. IBAs are designed to provide employment opportunities for the locally underemployed and unemployed populations. For communities with low education levels, IBAs often stipulate a role for the proponent to train the unemployed, facilitate their recruitment, and retain them over the long-term in career advancement positions. In the space below outline the skill level of the indigenous population and programs to make them employable in the proponent's industry. Also list arrangements for the indigenous unemployed after decommissioning at the bottom of table 14.1. Data from tables 8.6 and 8.7 will provide beginning information for the IBA. As shown in table 14.1, the assessor must obtain the titles and the number of jobs for each project and match that with the availability and skill level of persons in the impact community. These data must be added to the IBA agreement and used as the basis for monitoring.

Step 3. **Complete Table 14.1 Below Using Numbers from Proponent Proposal using SIA #11 to Assess Job Availability for impacted Communities (Snap Lake Diamond Mine in the Canadian NWT is our example)**

Job Descriptions from Proponent Proposal	Project Title #'s	Hourly Wage	# Available	Education Required ¥	Qualify Comm #1	Qualify Comm #2	Qualifed Total for all Communities
Equipment Operators	18			10/LIT/EX			
Plant Operators	16			10/LIT			
Paste Fill Man	14			10/LIT/EX			
Security Guards	8			12/GED			
Crusher/Grad Operts	12			10/LIT			
Development Miner	140			12/GED			
Scoop Truck Operts	22			10/LIT/EX			
Nippers	16			10/LIT			
Food Service	12			12/GED			
Maids/Janitors	8			8			
Construction/laborers	8			10/LIT			
Totals					Sum	Sum	Sum

¥ The education requirement is the number of years of formal education, LIT means able to speak and communicate in English, and EX means the position requires experience (including a GED).

Suggested or guaranteed employment after project decommissioning...............

....

....

Step 4: Provisions to provide independent business opportunities for persons in the impacted communities. IBAs could include provisions for indigenous business to provide goods and services to the approved development. In some cases this means that industry will agree to "unbundle" services and sourcing so that they can be bid on effectively by local business, or that indigenous business are given the opportunity to bid in advance of other service and materials providers. Use a format similar to Table 8.5 (page 84) in listing community and regional businesses that could benefit from the proposed development.

#1 _____

#2 _____

#3 _____

#4 _____

Step 5. Provisions to specify industry's social, cultural and community support to mitigate the negative impacts of resource development on the traditional lifestyle of the community. To address the negative impacts that mineral extraction activity may have on traditional life styles and culture of the impacted communities, IBAs often have provisions that require industry to provide social and community assistance for employees and their family; fund community and projects; and physical infrastructure and cultural activities both in and outside the workplace. In the space below write the amount, type and beneficiary of cash or in kind contributions for community infrastructure needs as shown on page 154 .

Community Infrastructure	Present Situation	Number with Project	Variance (+ or -)	Baseline Situation
Police/Sheriffs (2.1)	____	____	____	3.5
Patrol Cars (1.1)	____	____	____	2
Firefighters (1.5)	____	____	____	4.5
Medic Units (.25)	____	____	____	0

Step 6. Provisions to provide royalty benefits to Indigenous communities. Aboriginal, First Nation and Tribal groups may have land claim agreements that provide royalties from surface and/or subsurface mineral rights. However, these payments may also be established through separate royalty and land management arrangements. A state, provincial or federal government often collects and distributes these royalties. In the U.S., royalties from mineral development on Native American lands were collected by the Federal government. However, only in 2011 are royalties being distributed to Native American Tribes. If applicable, provide a legal reference and the provisions of any royalty arrangements in the spaces below.

1. Legal provisions for surface and sub-surface mineral rights...........................

....

2. Monitoring and collection agency for royalty benefits..............................

3.Methods and timetables for distribution of cash royalties to indigenous

communities...

4. Non-monetary distribution of benefits and royalties..............................

Step 6. Provisions to provide environmental protection and cultural resources. IBAs often include specific environmental protection and monitoring provisions. They protect the habitat for wildlife so that, for example, traditional hunting and fishing may continue. IBAs also protect areas of cultural and historical significance. For example, some IBAs stipulate that non-Aboriginal employees be forbidden from specified areas of religious significance. List below the procedures for restricting outside access to and knowledge of sacred areas. SIA variable #28 (page 133) could provide an empirical checklist for this component.

1.Protections provided by the project proponent.......................................

....

....

2. Protections provided by the impacted communities................................

....

....

Step 7. Procedural Provisions. IBAs need a series of provisions that deal with the mechanics of implementation. At a minimum, these must include a mechanism for creating, implementing and empowering committees, and a dispute resolution mechanism, ☛ Kenneth (1999). Make sure the SIMP and the IBA includes such a protocol. List those provisions below.

1. Dates for the beginning of the IBA_____

2. Protocols for implementation of the IBA_____

3.Authority and arbitrators for the enforcement of project disputes_____

Step 8. Citizens Advisory Board or Monitoring Board. This committee must ensure that the mitigation procedures that were identified in the mitigation and monitoring (Chapter 13) are actually being carried out. List below the expected composition of the Monitoring Board and who will respond to the findings and recommendations of a Citizen Member Advisory type board. See table on page 41 for example stakeholders.

Elected Community Leaders   **Indigenous Community Citizens/Organizations**

[   ]   [   ]

[   ]   [   ]

Governmental Legal Authorities   **Project Proponent**

[   ]   [   ]

Step 9. An enforcement agreement must include enforceable penalties if the components of the IBA were not carried out. Included in this enforcement agreement should be a mechanism for settling disputes as well as details on fines and criteria for initiating work stoppages. List below any Federal, State or Provincial legislation, if implemented or presently legislated, would ensure that the core components of the IBA would be enforced. Completing this step will require a review of land use legislation covering the project jurisdiction

Listing of Federal, State, regional , provincial or municipal legislation dealing with the enforcement of components of IBA agreements:

....

....

....

....

Why are Aboriginal People Skeptical?

This old lady was walking along, looking for berries and she found this gold rock. Later on, when a prospector saw the rock, he asked where she found it and said they wanted this rock. The old lady said: "No! You give me something and then I will give it to you." He gave her three stove pipes for that rock. That's how the gold mines came to be here [in Yellowknife, the Northwest Territory]. And our people did not benefit from that..as you see today, we walk around the arsenic that's left behind. Who's going to clean that up?

(Paraphrased from an interview by Lindsay Galbraith in Yellowknife, NWT (2005), used here with permission of the author)

Activity 14.3 Issues and Difficulties with Impacts and Benefits Agreements

Many of the problems listed on the following page come from comments by First Nations, U.S. Tribal Governments and other indigenous populations in their attempts to receive the benefits of resource development in their jurisdictions. Most of the experiences come from mineral development activity in areas of Canada, Western and Northern Australia, the United States, Mexico and South Africa.

1. **Legal language and legal enforcement**. The complexities and requirements of legal language must fit within the legal structure of the appropriate jurisdiction. That language is necessary to enforce any of the provisions of the IBA. Often, these documents are not translated to plain language and thereby misunderstood by some community members.

2. **Early involvement in decision making & resource management** The IBA is seldom mentioned or considered during the initial planning process and scoping, as detailed in Chapter 3.

3. **IBAs for social and financial impacts are seldom included with biophysical and health impacts**—health, environmental and social impacts are all part of an integrated impact assessment.

4. **Signatories (responsibility)** It is important to ensure that the parties that sign the IBA are legal representatives of both the impacted communities and the project proponent (industry).

5. **Often the IBA components are done in secretive negotiations.** Unfortunately, there are cases where industry negotiates with leaders that do not always represent the best interests of the impacted community. Therefore, IBAs must above all be transparent and understood by all members of the impacted communities. The EIA, SIA and Public consultation are by law and practice public processes.

6. **Socio, cultural and economic polarization** may occur within the impacted community if the benefits are not equally shared. In the case of ancillary business, all community members must have equal access to the opportunities. If, as part of the IBA, the proponent agrees to upgrade community infrastructure, there must be some control over the manner in which the funds are spent. Doing the community infrastructure and social services needs assessment as part of SIA variable number 26, will help guarantee that community priority needs are addressed.

7. **Mitigation must be directed at the community level and not focused at the individual level**. Benefits directed at the community level will lead to greater internal accountability and reduce the misuse of proponent funds.

8. **Agreement on data to collect**. Monitoring provisions from Chapter 13 are key to making sure that the terms of the IBA are actually being carried out. Agreement is needed in advance on the type of data to be collected, who will collect it, and how widely the results will be shared.

9. **Lack of follow-up** An Impacts and Benefits Agreement involves a lot of trust both by the proponent and the community. The enforceable components of the agreement need to be such that only follow-up by the Citizen Advisory Committee is necessary for rectification. It is not an easy situation. However, with a signed IBA in place, industry should benefit from a stable workforce and a supportive community. The community will benefit from stable family incomes and a functioning local government.

10. **Citizen burn-out** may be a problem if the community members serving on Citizen Advisory Committees or doing data collection are volunteers. Term limits and a succession procedure may help!

Activity 14.4 The Future of Impacts and Benefits Agreements

- There is a need for the regulatory and judicial components of the public sector to become engaged in Impact and Benefits Agreements related to natural resource developments not only in Aboriginal and Indigenous Territories, but on both public and private lands. The absence of any sort of regulatory framework around the negotiations of IBAs, including content and timelines, increases uncertainty for extractive industries in an already highly uncertain environment. Meantime, impacted communities need a greater public sector presence in the IBA process so that they can deliver to their citizens an effective benefits package.

- IBAs are not and should not be about resource revenue sharing. Industry is in the business of wealth creation and it is the role of the public sector to be concerned about how that wealth is distributed.

- All levels of government need a clear policy statement on how revenues acquired by way of IBAs will be treated vis-à-vis program transfer payments.

- There needs to be a policy discussion and conclusion on the role of local governments in the regulatory process--be they Tribal, First Nations, Federal, Provincial, Municipal or County.

- The environmental assessment process requires substantial clarification regarding how mitigation and monitoring should proceed. At present social and financial issues are tangential to environmental impact assessment in most countries with NEPA style legislation. Industry needs implementation certainty of how mitigation components are identified in the environmental assessment process. - Chapter 12.

- Federal governments in partnership with the relevant state and provincial governments must support Aboriginal and Indigenous communities in the regional planning processes aimed at: defining development opportunities and constraints including mapping of traditional pursuits and areas of cultural significance; identifying educational and training needed to prepare for economic opportunities; and the provision and timing of physical and social infrastructure related to development opportunities.

▪   Environmental assessment agencies must expand their role in assisting communities (both indigenous and otherwise) to ensure that they have adequate resources including building human resource capacity (social capital) to undertake community social impact assessments and consultations related to natural resource projects and other development.

▪   Rather than leave social and financial monitoring and adjustment to IBA negotiations, (or environmental assessment processes), all levels of government must cooperate to develop and implement a comprehensive social and financial management plan in regions subject to major present and proposed natural resource developments. Long term monitoring indicators that include cumulative social and environmental effects must be included.

▪   All levels of governments must undertake policy consultations with industry to consider whether IBAs should become a requirement to receive regulatory approval/licensing for a major resource development and if so, what parameters for IBAs should be defined. Guidelines for corporate social and environmental responsibility, when implemented should consider such matters as: 1) when an IBA is required; 2) the interested and effected parties to an agreement and means of determining the Aboriginal and indigenous communities; 3) content requirements including definitions of impacts and benefits to be included; 4) engagement of appropriate government agencies for program interfaces to implement defined benefits; 5) timelines for negotiations; 6) resources for negotiations (public and private sector); 7) dispute resolution in the negotiation process; 8) ratification procedures, and implementation measures including monitoring and dispute resolution.

▪   The environmental assessment process must be clarified in terms of expectations respecting social and financial impacts and monitoring to include only those aspects that are specifically within the influence and control of the developer of a proposed project and not subject to other social forces.

This chapter draws extensively from a paper by ⌕ Gordon Shanks, March, 2006. "*Sharing the Benefits of Resource Development: A Study of First Nations-Industry Impact Benefits Agreements,*" Public Policy Forum, 1405-130 Albert Street, Ottawa, ON KIP 564. Accessed at www.ppforum.ca and used here by permission of the Public Policy Forum.

The last section includes a bibliography and suggested web sites.

Social Impact Assessment Bibliography and References

The enclosed reference list is limited to English language serialized scholarly and professional journals, retrievable government documents and bulletins as well as books and monographs with an ISBN number. *Gray Literature*, e.g., papers, meeting presentations and proceedings and documents with limited distribution are not included. Articles and chapters in special issues of journals and books are not cited separately **if the entire issue or volume is devoted to social impact assessment**.

Textbooks and Guides to SIA

Barrow, C. J. 2000. *Social Impact Assessment: An Introduction*. London, Arnold.

Burdge, Rabel J. 2015. *A Community Guide to Social Impact Assessment: 2015 Training Course Edition*. https://securereg.mauconsulting.ca/iasnr/index.php?L1=left_home.php&L2=body_bookorder.php International association for Society and Natural Resources. http://www.iasnr.org

International Association for Impact Assessment (IAIA). 2003. International Principles for Social Impact Assessment. *Impact Assessment and Project Appraisal*, 21(1)5-11. Go to **www.iaia.org/** and click on publications for pdf files of these documents.

IOCGP, Interorganizational Committee on Principles and Guidelines for Social Impact Assessment. 2003. U. S. Principles and Guidelines for Social Impact Assessment. *Impact Assessment and Project Appraisal*, 21(3):233-270. Go to **www.iaia.org/** and click on publications.

Taylor, Nicholas C., Hobson Bryan and Colin Goodrich. 2004. *Social Assessment: Theory, Process and Techniques: 3rd Edition*. Taylor, Baines and Associates, Christchurch, New Zealand. Order at books@tba.co.nz

Vanclay, F. (ed) 2014. *Developments in Social Impact Assessment*. Cheltenham, UK: Edward Elgar.

Regulations, Content and Administrative Procedures

Bass, Ronald. 1998. Evaluating Environmental Justice under the National Environmental Policy Act. *Environmental Impact Assessment Review*, 18(1): 32-92.

Council on Environment Quality (CEQ). 1997. *Considering Cumulative Effects under the National Policy Act*. Washington, D.C., Office of the President. Down load at: **http://ceq.eh.doe.gov/nepa/nepanet.htm**

Council on Environment Quality (CEQ). 1997. *Environmental Justice: Guidance under the National Environmental Policy Act*. Washington, D.C., Office of the President. Down load at: **http://ceq.eh.doe.gov/nepa/regs/ej/justice.pdf**

Donnelly, Annie, Barry Dalal-Clayton and Ross Hughes. 1998. *A Directory of Impact Assessment Guidelines, Second Edition*, Bookshop Manager, IIED, 3 Endsleigh St. London, WC1H 0DD, United Kingdom.

Executive Office of the President of the United States. 1994. Executive Order 12898: Federal Actions to Address Environmental Justice in Minority Populations and Low-Income Populations. *Federal Register*, 59: pp 7629 et seq.

Francis, Paul and Susan Jacobs. 1999. Institutionalising Social Analysis at the World Bank. *Environmental Impact Assessment Review*, 19(3):341-357.

Gamble, D.J. 1978. The Berger Inquiry: An Impact Assessment Process. *Science*, 199(3) 946-952.

Llewellyn, Lynn G. and William R. Freudenburg. 1989. Legal Requirements for Social Impact Assessment: Assessing the Social Science Fallout from Three Mile Island. *Society and Natural Resources*, 2(3): 193-208.

NEPA. National Environmental Policy Act of 1969. *Public Law* 91-190:852-859.42, U.S.C. and as amended *Public Law* 94-52 and 94-83. 42, U.S.C., pp 4321-4347.

U.S. Council on Environment Quality. 1986. *Regulations for Implementing the Procedural Provisions of the National Environmental Policy Act* (40 CFR 1500-1508). Washington: Government Printing Office, Washington, D.C. 20402. **http://ceq.eh.doe.gov/nepa/nepanet.htm**

United States and Canadian Agencies and Ministries Social Impact Assessment and Related Social Assessment Procedures

McCold, L. N. and J. W. Saulsbury. 1998. Defining the No-Action Alternative for National Environmental Policy Act Analysis of Continuing Actions. *Environmental Impact Assessment Review*, 18: 353-370.

U.S. Agency for International Development. (USAID).1978. *AID Handbook.* U.S. Government Printing Office, Washington, DC pp. 4A- I to 4A- I 1.

U.S. Bureau of Reclamation (USDI). 2001. *Social Analysis Manuel Volume I: Manager's Guide to Using Social Analysis*; *Volume II Social Analyst's Guide to Doing Social Analysis*. Resource Management and Planning Group. Technical Service Center, Denver Federal Center D-8580, Bldg. 67. Denver, CO 80225-0007.

U.S. Department of Transportation. 1996. FHWA-PD-96-036 HEP-30/8-96 (10M)P: Community Impact Assessment—A Quick Reference for Transportation (September). **http://www.environment.fhwa.dot.gov/projdev/td mcia.asp**

U.S. Department of Transportation. Federal Highway Administration. May 1998. *Community Impact Mitigation: Case Studies*. Publication No. FHWA-PD-98-024.

U.S. Forest Service. 1982. Guidelines for Economic and Social Analysis of Programs, Resource Plans, and Projects: Final Policy, *Federal Register,* 47(80) April 26, pp. 17940-17954.

U.S. Office of Management and Budget. 2002. Guidelines for Ensuring and Maximizing the Quality, Objectivity, Utility, and Integrity of Information Disseminated by Federal Agencies. *Federal Register,* 67 (36).

Water Resources Council. 1983. *Economic and Environmental Principles and Guidelines for Water and Related Land Resources Implementation Studies*. U.S. Government Printing Office. Washington, DC.

State-of-the-Art and Literature Reviews

Burdge, Rabel J. and Frank Vanclay. 1995. Social Impact Assessment: State of the Art. *Impact Assessment*, 14(1):57-86.

Burdge, Rabel J. 2002. Why is Social Impact Assessment the Orphan of the Assessment Process? *Impact Assessment and Project Appraisal*, 20(1):3-9.

Esteves, A.M., Franks, D.M. & Vanclay, F. 2012. Social Impact Assessment: The State of the Art. *Impact Assessment and Project Appraisal* 30(1): 35-44.

Finsterbusch, Kurt. 1995. In Praise of SIA: A Personal Review of the Field of Social Impact Assessment. *Impact Assessment*, 13(3):229-52.

Freudenburg, William R. 1986. Social Impact Assessment. *Annual Review of Sociology*, 12:451-478.

Lockie, S.F. 2001. SIA in Review: Setting the Agenda for Impact Assessment in the 21st Century. *Impact Assessment and Project Appraisal* 19(4): 277-287.

Vanclay, F. & Esteves, A.M. (eds) 2011. N*ew Directions in Social Impact Assessment: Conceptual and Methodological Advances*. Cheltenham, UK: Edward Elgar.

Conceptual Guidelines for Social Impact Assessment

Becker, Henk A. and Frank Vanclay. eds. 2002. *The International Handbook of Social Impact Assessment.* Cheltenham, Colchester, United Kingdom: Edward Elgar Publishing.

Burdge, Rabel J. 2004. *The Concepts, Process and Methods of Social Impact Assessment.* Social Ecology Press, 210 E Sherwin Drive, Urbana, 61802, USA. burdge@comcast.net For the Chinese translation see—ISBN 978-7-5111-0612-4

Freudenburg, William R. and Robert Gramling. 1992. Community Impacts of Technological Change: Toward a Longitudinal Perspective. *Social Forces,* 70(4): 937-55.

Goldman, L.R. (ed) 2000. *Social Impact Analysis: An Applied Anthropology Manual.* Oxford: Berg.

Freudenburg, William R. and Susan K. Pastor. 1992. Public Responses to Technological Risks: Toward a Sociological Perspective. *Sociological Quarterly,* 33(3, August): 389-412.

Freudenburg, William R. and Kenneth M. Keating. 1985. Applying Sociology to Policy: Social Science and the Environmental Impact Statement. *Rural Sociology,* 50(4):578-605.

Gramling, Robert and William R. Freudenburg. 1992. Opportunity-Threat, Development, and Adaptation: Toward a Comprehensive Framework for Social Impact Assessment. *Rural Sociology,* 57(2):216-234.

Rickson, Roy E., Rabel J. Burdge and Audrey Armour. eds. 1990. Integrating Impact Assessment into the Planning Process: International Perspectives and Experience. *Impact Assessment Bulletin,* 8: (1/2); 357 pages.

Slootweg, R., Vanclay, F. and van Schooten, M. 2001. Function Evaluation as a Framework for the Integration of Social and Environmental Impact Assessment. *Impact Assessment and Project Appraisal,* 19(1):19-28.

Vanclay, Frank. 2001. Conceptualising Social Impacts. *Environmental Impact Assessment Review,* 22(3):183-211.

Vanclay, Frank and D. A. Bronstein. eds. 1995. *Environmental and Social Impact Assessment.* Chichester, Sussex, UK: Wiley & Sons.

Wolf, C.P. 1980. Getting Social Impact Assessment into the Policy Arena, *Environmental Impact Assessment Review,* 1(1):27-36.

SIA Methodology

Cernea, Michael M. 1994. Using Knowledge from Social Sciences in Development Projects. *Project Appraisal, 9(2):83-94.*

Bruce Harvey & Sara Bice (2014) Social impact assessment, social development programmes and social license to operate: tensions and contradictions in intent and practice in the extractive sector, *Impact Assessment and Project Appraisal,* 32:4, 327-335

Chambers, Robert. 1994. The Origins and Practice of Participatory Rural Appraisal. *World Development,* 22(7): 953-969.

Conyers, Diane. 1993. Guidelines on Social Analysis for Rural Area Development Planning. FAO: Rome. *Training Manual No. 73.*

Dale, Alan, C. Nicholas Taylor and Marcus Lane. eds. 2001. *Social Assessment in Natural Resource Management Institutions.* Collingwood, Victoria, Australia: CSIRO Publishing. **http://www.publish.csiro.au/books/**

Denq, Furjen and June Altenhofel. 1997. Social Impact Assessments Conducted by Federal Agencies: An Evaluation. *Impact Assessment,* 15: 209-231.

Feeney, Rachel Gallant (2013) Evaluating the use of social impact assessment in Northeast US federal fisheries management, *Impact Assessment and Project Appraisal,* 31:4, 271-279

Franks, D.M. & Vanclay, F. 2013. Social Impact Management Plans: Innovation in Corporate and Public Policy. *Environmental Impact Assessment Review* 43: 40-48.

Finsterbusch, Kurt, J. Ingersol, and Lynn Llewellyn. eds. 1990. *Methods for Social Analysis in Developing Countries.* Boulder, CO: Westview Press.

Franks, D.M. & Vanclay, F. 2013. Social Impact Management Plans: Innovation in Corporate and Public Policy. *Environmental Impact Assessment Review* 43: 40-48.

Goodrich, Colin and C. Nicholas Taylor. Guest eds. 1995. Special Issue on Social Assessment. *Project Appraisal*, 10:3, 141-196.

Halstead, John M., Robert A. Chase, Steve H. Murdock and F. Larry Leistritz. 1985. *Socioeconomic Impact Management: Design and Implementation.* Boulder, CO: Westview Press, 250 pages.

Franks, D. and F. Vanclay. 2013. Social Impact Management Plans: Innovation in corporate and public policy. *Environmental Impact Assessment Review* 43:40-48.

International Association for Impact Assessment. 1995. *Principles of Environmental Impact Assessment: Best Practices*. 1330 23rd Street South, Suite C. Fargo, ND 58103. Accessed at: **http://www.iaia.org/**

King, Thomas F. 1998. How the Anthropologists Stole Culture: A Gap in American Environmental Impact Assessment Practice and How to Fill It. *Environmental Impact Assessment Review*, 18(2): 117-134.

Leistritz, Larry and Steven H. Murdock. 1981. *The Socioeconomic Impact of Resource Development: Methods of Assessment*, Boulder, CO: Westview Press.

McCold, Lance N. and James W. Saulsbury. 1998. Defining the No-Action Alternative for National Environmental Policy Act Analysis of Continuing Actions. *Environmental Impact Assessment Review*, 18: 15-38.

Mulvihill, Peter R. and Peter Jacobs. 1998. Using Scoping as a Design Process. *Environmental Impact Assessment Review*, 18: 350-370.

Nish S, Bice S. 2011. Community based agreement-making with land connected peoples. In: Vanclay F, Esteves AM, editors. *New directions in social impact assessment: Conceptual and methodological advances.* Cheltenham: Edward Elgar; p. 59–78.

O'Faircheallaigh, Ciaran. 1999. Making Social Impact Assessment Count: A Negotiation-Based Approach for Indigenous Peoples. *Society and Natural Resources*, 12(1), pp 63-80.

Rickson, Roy E., Tor Hundloe, Geoffrey T. McDonald and Rabel J. Burdge. Eds. 1990. Social Impact of Development: Putting Theory and Methods into Practice. *Environmental Impact Assessment Review*, 10(1/2): 357 pages.

Seebohm, Kym. 1997. Guiding Principles for the Practice of Social Assessment in the Australian Water Industry. *Impact Assessment*, 15: 233-251. Stoffle, Richard W., et al. 1990. Calculating the Cultural Significance of American Indian Plants: Paiute and Shoshone Ethnobotany at Yucca Mountain Nevada. *American Anthropologist*, 92(2): 416-432.

Svetla Petrova & Dora Marinova (2015) Using 'soft' and 'hard' social impact indicators to understand societal change caused by mining: a Western Australia case study, *Impact Assessment and Project Appraisal*, 33:1, 16-27.

Stolp, A., W. Groen, et al. 2002. Citizen Values Assessment: Incorporating Citizen's Value Judgments in Environmental Impact Assessment. *Impact Assessment and Project Appraisal*, 20(1): 11-23.

SIA Research Findings

Brealey, T. B., C. C. Neil and P. W. Newton. eds. *Resource Communities: Settlement and Workforce Issues.* CSIRO Publications. East Melbourne, Victoria, Australia.

Burdge, Rabel J. Guest editor. 2003. The Practice of Social Impact Assessment: Part I. *Impact Assessment and Project Appraisal*, 21(2): 81-160. **www.scipol.demon.co.uk/iapa.htm**

Burdge, Rabel J. Guest editor. 2003. The Practice of Social Impact Assessment: Part II. *Impact Assessment and Project Appraisal*, 21(3): 166-250. **www.scipol.demon.co.uk/iapa.htm**

Burnigham, K. 1995. Attitudes, Accounts and Impact Assessment. *The Sociological Review*, 43(1): 100-122.

Cochrane, Glynn. 1979. *The Cultural Appraisal of Development Projects*. New York: Praeger Publications.

Cernea, Michael M. ed. 1991. *Putting People First: Sociological Variables in Rural Development 2nd Edition*. New York: Oxford University Press.

Dixon, Mim. 1978. *What Happened to Fairbanks: The Effects of the Trans-Alaska Oil Pipeline on the Community of Fairbanks, Alaska*. Boulder, CO: Westview Press.

Egre, D. & Senecal, P. 2003. Social Impact Assessments of Large Dams Throughout the World: Lessons Learned Over Two Decades. *Impact Assessment and Project Appraisal* 21(3): 215-224.

Elkind-Savatsky, Pamela. 1986. *Differential Social Impacts of Rural Resource Development*. Boulder, CO: Westview Press. 293 pp.

Freudenburg, William R. and Kenneth M. Keating. 1985. Applying Sociology to Policy: Social Science and the Environmental Impact Statement. *Rural Sociology*, 50(4):578-605.
Freudenburg, William R. and Robert Gramling. 1992. Community Impacts of Technological Change: Toward a Longitudinal Perspective. *Social Forces*, 70(4): 937-55.

Freudenburg, William R. and Robert Gramling. 1994. *Oil in Troubled Waters: Perceptions, Politics and the Battle over Offshore Drilling*. State University Press of New York, Albany.

Freudenburg, William R. and Robert E. Jones. 1992. Criminal Behavior and Rapid Community Growth: Examining the Evidence. *Rural Sociology*, 56 (4): 619-45.

Freudenburg, William R., Richard L. Perrine, and F. Roach, eds., 1984. *Paradoxes of Western Energy Development*. Boulder, CO: Westview.

Goldman, Laurence R. ed. 2000. *Social Impact Analysis: An Applied Anthropology Manuel*. London: Berg, Oxford: University Press.

Gramling, Robert and William R. Freudenburg. 1990. A Closer Look at `Local Control: Communities, Commodities, and the Collapse of the Coast. *Rural Sociology*, 55(4): 541-58.

Greider, Thomas and Lorraine Garkovich. 1994. Symbolic Landscapes: The Social Construction of Nature and the Environment. *Rural Sociology*, 59 (1) 1-24.

Hunter, Lori M., Richard S. Krannich and Michael D. Smith. 2002. Rural Migration, Rapid Growth, and Fear of Crime. *Rural Sociology,* 67(1):71-89.

Murdock, Steven H., Richard S. Krannich and F. Larry Leistritz. 1999. *Hazardous Wastes in Rural America: Impacts Implications and Options for Rural Communities*. Lanham, Maryland: Rowman & Littlefield.

O'Faircheallaigh, C. 2009. Effectiveness in Social Impact Assessment: Aboriginal Peoples and Resource Development in Australia. I*mpact Assessment and Project Appraisal* 27(2): 95-110.

Pakin, V.1996. When Science is Not Enough: A Case Study in Social Impact Mitigation. *Impact Assessment*, 14(3): 321-328.

Rickson, Roy E. Marcus Lane, Mark Lynch-Blosse, John Western. 1995. Community, Environment and Development: Social Impact Assessment in Resource-Dependent Communities. *Impact Assessment*, 13(4):347-386.

Smith, Michael D., Richard S. Krannich, and Lori M. Hunter. 2001. Growth, Decline, Stability, and Disruption: A Longitudinal Analysis of Social Well-Being in Four Western Rural Communities. *Rural Sociology,* 66(3):425-450.

Stoffle, Richard W. et al. 1991. Risk Perception Mapping: Using Ethnography to Define the Locally Affected Population for a Low-Level Radioactive Waste Storage Facility in Michigan. *American Anthropologist*, 93 (3): 611-635.

Stoffle, Richard W. and Richard Arnold. 2003. Confronting the Angry Rock: American Indians' Situated Risks from Radioactivity. *Ethnos*, 68(2):230-248.

Thompson, James G. and Gary Williams. 1990. Vertical Linkage and Competition for Local Political Power: A Case of Natural Resource Development and Federal Land Power. *Impact Assessment,* 10(4): 33-58.

Public Involvement and Social Impact Assessment

Buchan, Dianne. 2003. Buy-in and Social Capital: By-Products of Social Impact Assessment. *Impact Assessment and Project Appraisal*, 2(3): 168-172.

Howell, R.E., M.E. Olsen, and D. Olsen. 1987. *Designing a Citizen Involvement Program.* Corvallis, OR: Western Rural Development Center, WREP 105.

O'Connor Center for the Rocky Mountain West. 2000. *Reclaiming NEPAs Potential: Can Collaborative Processes Improve Environmental Decision Making?* Missoula, MT: O'Connor Center for the Rocky Mountain West, University of Montana 59812-3096. To order click on **http://www.crmw.org/** and go to publications.

Roberts, Richard 1995. Public Involvement: From Consultation to Participation. In Vanclay and Bronstein eds. *Environmental and Social Impact Assessment*, pp 221-246.

Vining, Joanne. Guest ed. 1988. Public Involvement in Natural Resource Management. *Society and Natural Resources*, 1(4) entire issue.

World Bank. 1996. Guidelines for Using Social Assessment to Support Public Involvement in World Bank--GEF Projects. World Bank, Environmental Department, Global Environment Division: Washington, D.C.

Peer Reviewed Journals

American Anthropologist **www.aaanet.org/**

Australian Geographical Studies **www.iag.org.au**

Environmental Impact Assessment Review Alan.Bond@uea.ac.uk editor) or for copy **http://www.journals.elsevier.com/environmental-impact-assessment-review/**

Human Organization Submit at **www.humanorg.org**

Impact Assessment and Project Appraisal (formerly *Impact Assessment Bulletin*, shortened to *Impact Assessment* and combined with *Project Appraisal* in 1998). Go to the IAIA website **www.iaia.org**

Rural Sociology **www.ruralsociology.org**

Society and Natural Resources go to editor **carroll@wsu.edu** For a sample copy send to: **snr@tandfpa.com**

Journal of Environmental Assessment Policy and Management. **w.sheate@imperial.ac.uk** For a sample copy go to: **http://ejournals.wspc.com.sg/cgi-bin/printed_copy.cgi?jeapm**

Journal of Environmental Management and Planning Editor is **Ken.Willis@ncl.ac.uk** For a sample copy go to: **http://www.tandf.co.uk/journals/titles/09640568.asp**

Web sites for International Professional Associations on Environmental and Social Impact Assessment

-The-International Association for Impact Assessment was organized in 1981 to bring together researchers, government employees, practitioners, and users of all types of impact assessment. **www.iaia.org** for purchasing *Impact Assessment and Project Appraisal* and joining IAIA.

-International Association for Society and Resource Management **http://www.iasnr.org/**

-International Association for Public Participation (IAP2) was established in 1990 to serve as a focal point for networking about public involvement. The journal is *Interact: the Journal of Public Participation*—**www.iap2.org**

-National Association of Environmental Professionals work on a variety of environmental planning issues. They publish *The Environmental Professional.* **www.naep.org**

-Home page of the New Zealand Association for Impact Assessment (NZAIA). **http://www.nzaia.org.nz/**

International Council for Mines and Metals (ICMM). 2010. Good practice guide: Indigenous peoples and mining. London: ICMM, [accessed 2014 July 1]. Available from:
http://www.icmm.com/document/1221
International Council for Mines and Metals

The Pacific and Business Law Institute of Vancouver, B.C. offers conferences and courses on various contractual relationships between private sector mining companies and First Go to:
http://www.pbli.com/conferences

-The website of the Western and Northern Canada Affiliate Office of the IAIA. Details on their activities, conferences, publications and membership.
http://www.iaia-wnc.ca/

-The website of AQEI—Quebec Association for Environmental Evaluation. Includes references in French, English and Spanish.
http://www.aqei.qc.ca/

Country Specific Environmental and Social Impact Assessment Web Sites

-US Council on Environmental Quality has NEPA regulations, scoping procedures, and links to regulations in key US land management agencies. EIA analysis includes socio-economic information.
http://ceq.eh.doe.gov/nepa/nepanet.htm or
http://tis.eh.doe.gov/nepa/tools/tools.htm or
http://tis.eh.doe.gov/nepa/docs/docs.htm

-Home page of the Canadian Environmental Assessment Agency. Details on the Act, procedures, steps and a variety of links.
http://www.ceaa-acee.gc.ca/index_e.htm

-Australian EIA Network has information on environmental impact assessment (EIA) and its process within Australia.
http://www.environment.gov.au/

-Website of the Yukon Environmental Assessment Board. Includes electronic copies of their many publications and recent SEIA guidelines.
http://www.yesab.ca/publications/guides.html

-The New Zealand Ministry of the Environment has a range of information on recent publications and can be ordered on line through this link.
http://www.mfe.govt.nz

-Website of the Mackenzie Valley Environmental Impact Review Board. Includes electronic copies of their new SEIA Guidelines as well as all documents related to their project related assessments.
http://www.mveirb.nt.ca

-Community Impact assessment is the homepage of the Federal Department of Transportation and the Florida Department of Transportation
http://www.environment.fhwa.dot.gov/projdev/td mcia.asp

-The World Bank--publication on social analysis, their term for social impact Assessment, is at:
www.worldbank.org/socialanalysissourcebook/

For additional information on World Bank publications. Go to:
http://www.publications.worldbank.org/

-Asian Development Bank. Checklists on gender analysis at: **www.adb.org/gender/checklists.asp** For topics such as Education, Agriculture, Water supply and sanitation, Urban development and housing go to: **http://www.adb.org/Publications/default.asp**

The Concepts, Process and Methods of Social Impact Assessment
(Available only on line and translated into Chinese in 2009)
By Rabel J. Burdge

INTRODUCING SOCIAL IMPACT ASSESSMENT